SUGA WATER

SUGA WATER

A MEMOIR
ARSHAY COOPER

WISE Ink
CREATIVE ★ PUBLISHING

This is a work of creative nonfiction. The events are portrayed to the best of Arshay Cooper's memory. While all the stories in this book are true, some names and identifying details have been changed to protect the privacy of the people involved.

ISBN: 978-1-940014-61-6
eISBN: 978-1-940014-64-7

Library of Congress Catalog Number: 2015936940
Printed in the United States of America
First Printing: 2015
19   18   17   16   15   5   4   3   2   1

Cover design by Jessie Sayward Bright
Interior design by Kim Morehead

WISE Ink
CREATIVE * PUBLISHING

Wise Ink Creative Publishing
Minneapolis, MN 55405
www.wiseinkpub.com

To order, visit www.itascabooks.com or call 1-800-901-3480.
Reseller discounts available.

*This book is dedicated to
my mother Linda who represents hope,
and to the city of Chicago who's in search for it.*

PART 1
WEST SIDE

Growing up, we had a fan in our apartment that one day started making a loud clicking noise. We couldn't afford a new one, so we kept it. After a while, the clicking noise didn't bother us, almost like it wasn't there. We only remembered when new people visited and reminded us of the noise. That's how the violence in our city is during the summer. So many people are getting beat up, shot, and killed that it doesn't bother people as much as it used to, only when the news makes it a big deal.

There are zombies in every direction. That's what I call the drug addicts in the hallway of our building. My mother used to be one of them. My aunts and uncles were too.

Their arms are usually the first thing I notice, always clawing for something. Their eyes have no soul, like life has been sucked out of them. They are as thin as drinking straws and speak no words, only noises. I'm petrified every time I tiptoe past them. The stairs groan with each step and I inhale the smell of drywall in the hallway to block the noise from my ears. When I get to the first floor, I put the key into our door and hear Sam Cooke playing, which means something is wrong. Bad news is like a storm; you feel it on your skin.

I walk into my room, close the door, and lie back and stare at the ceiling. My mind wanders for about five minutes and then the door opens. My mother has a look in her eyes that I have never seen. In my head, all I can think is, "Who died?" I am fifteen years old, sitting on my bed waiting for my mother to speak. If she had light skin, her face would be red. She is rocking back and forth with her hands shaking atop one another. It sounds like the radio is getting louder, but I know it isn't. I can hear the song saying, "...that he loves me and he cares." Who loves me and who cares? Looking back at my mom, I see her pupils floating in tears. She speaks and my life is forever changed.

"Arshay, my father, your grandfather, raped and beat me when I was younger."

She says there were times he had that look in his eyes for her little sisters too, but every time she saw him look at them she lunged, because there was no way she was going to let him touch her sisters.

"I was the oldest and it was my duty to be a big sister."

Suddenly, the noise on the radio doesn't exist. My body shuts down, but my mind is on high alert. My head sweats. I feel as if my heart is pierced with a sword. I keep staring at this woman, my mother, staring right into her eyes, and I can see all her hurt and feel all her feelings. I don't know what she wants me to say. I ask myself how many other families go through this. Is it normal for innocent young girls to be raped by their fathers? For God's sake, I'm only fifteen—why is she telling me? She was probably around my age when it happened, so how did this happen to her?

If she wants me to say something, she is disappointed because I say nothing. She gets up to walk away.

"You deserve to know."

I want to hug her, but we are not an affectionate family. I can't do what I don't know how to do. So I just sit there in our one-bedroom apartment shared by the five of us: me, my mother Linda, oldest brother Shaundell, younger brother Isaac, and little sister Pamela. I begin seeing things I hadn't before. I notice the stain on the wall that looks like Abraham Lincoln's face, the rust on the bunk bed that looks like a string of ponds, the creaky wooden floors, the missing slats in the blinds, seven nail holes in the wall.

I start thinking about a time at my grandfather's house years ago, when I was maybe nine years old, and he pushed through the door drunk, yelling, "I am the warlord! I am the G!" He was a very big man. My grandmother came into the kitchen in her nightgown, telling him to calm down and cut the noise out. He grabbed her and tried to rip her gown off as he dropped his pants to force himself on her. My grandmother was screaming, so Shaundell jumped on my grandfather's back and I started pushing him off her as she was hitting him upside the head with a boot. My grandmother pushed him towards the stove, which had all the burners lit—it was how we got heat. I saw my grandfather put his hand onto the grate, directly over the flame. I got scared, so I tried to pull him off but couldn't move his arm. I put my arm under his to keep him from burning. I didn't scream, but I do remember thinking to myself that even though my grandfather was a bad man, I had saved his life. I also felt like I was cursed with weakness because he deserved to burn. My grandfather eventually passed out.

Remembering that incident alone, I can only imagine what my mother went through. She leaves the room, and I play out a scene in my head of finding my grandfather and killing him, but he is already dead from a stroke.

An hour later, my brother Shaundell gets home. I am lying in bed scared with my eyes shut tight, my heart in my stomach, and my ears wide open. My mother is telling Shaundell exactly what she told me. I hear her ask him through tears, "Do you hate me?"

"No, ma."

And he cries like I never heard him cry before. We have been beaten with hands, cords, belts, and sticks, beaten until we cry ourselves to sleep, but I have never heard him cry like this. He doesn't stop crying, can't stop. I am not sure if he is crying out of anger, but I don't have the heart to ask, so I will myself to sleep.

....

At 6:00 a.m. my alarm goes off. I jump up quickly, as if last night was a bad dream. My mom shouts out to us, "Time to get up and pray!"

She is clapping her hands and singing:

He that believeth
he that believeth
have an everlasting life.
He that believeth
in the Father and the Son
have an everlasting life.
When I get to heaven
I'm gonna walk all around
have an everlasting life.
When I get to heaven
I'm gonna put on my crown
have everlasting life.

My younger brother Isaac complains about having to wake up so early to this noise.

"As for me and my house, we serve the Lord," she claims. Shaundell is quiet, his head down, not saying a word. My mom and I both know he just needs time. Maybe after school he will open up a bit.

Morning devotion is a daily routine in our apartment Monday through Sunday. We wake up to my mom's songs, we complain a little, and then we fight to get into the bathroom. We each have to find a scripture to read out loud, we sing a song (usually "Amazing Grace" or "God Will Make a Way"), and my mother asks if we have a prayer request. Afterward, we get on our knees and pray for a half hour. Most of the time, we just fall back to sleep, but if we get caught we have to stand the whole time. The weird thing is that sometimes my siblings will pray, sometimes they won't, but you can always tell one from the other. The sibling who prayed always felt good afterwards and minded their own business.

My mom has her rules, but she is fresh out of the Victory Outreach Recovery Home after well over a year. My brothers are already lost to the streets and their own desires. There wasn't always prayer in our home, but there was always a past.

....

There are no pictures of me from before the age of thirteen; drugs took them. There are no memories of kisses goodnight or the smell of breakfast in the morning; rock cocaine's to blame. There are no good grades, no junior high sweethearts, no ability to be popular at school, and no sense of belonging, thanks to alcohol abuse. This was not my addiction, but my mother's, and bitterness was stamped on the tablet of my heart.

At thirteen, I did something I regret. I chose to believe my mom was dead, even though I knew she wasn't. I had a funeral in my heart. I knew she was going to die in the streets. She was losing so much weight, she stole our Christmas gifts, and she would only come home two or three days a week. When she came home, she would cry aloud in the middle of the night and scream for her fix. I didn't know who she was anymore. She would dress herself in so many layers, one on top of the other, and when I saw her in the streets she was always with a different guy.

I counted her out. I didn't respect her and treated her like a dead woman roaming the streets. I didn't really know my dad and figured he left my mom for the same reason I wanted to leave, so I was bitter and blamed her. I have heard of other parents in our neighborhood dying from overdoses, and my mom seemed far worse than they'd been. I wanted to prepare myself mentally and emotionally for when my mother left us because of drugs, so I could be strong for my brothers and sister. I reached inside and decided she was already gone. It was the same feeling you get when the police or state troopers are behind you and it's only a matter of time before they stop you. I stopped thinking about her, I stopped worrying about her, but I still cried because I loved her too much and knew she couldn't stop. She had four kids she loved, so she would stop if she could, right? She was all I ever wanted and needed, but I felt like I had to be strong at thirteen. I wouldn't stay up at night waiting for her to come home with her usual hysterics just so I could fall asleep afterward.

A week passed with no sign of her. Two weeks, no mom. I was annoyed because she got a check and was supposed to buy us clothes. Three weeks, no sign, and I thought to myself that maybe she was gone. I was worried, but not upset. It was as though my heart went cold. We were all living with my grandmother at the time, and after a month passed, there was finally a call. My grandmother said that my mother had checked into a rehab home called Victory Outreach and wanted us to visit. I figured it wouldn't last. Six months passed. My brothers and sister would visit, but I never did. I didn't want to see her. They didn't know that she was dead to me.

··

A month later, around Thanksgiving of 1995, I found myself on the corner of 26th and Karlov Street, a wild Mexican neighborhood. The Two Six gang was hanging on the corner, and I wondered what was going on. If you are black and live in the West Side of Chicago, you know you do not cross the viaduct into the Mexican neighborhood. This is where the police drop you off when you mouth off to them and try to be a tough guy; it's like being dropped off in the middle of the ocean.

It was a cold day in Chicago, and my grandmother fought with me until I agreed to go to the Victory Outreach service. I guess my mom was sweating her to make sure I came. When we entered the building, there was beautiful music, different than anything I had ever heard. There were pictures of people of different ethnicities along the wall leading up the stairs. There was a black man and a white woman at the front door to the sanctuary, greeting me with a big smile. When I entered, everyone had their hands lifted. There were blacks, whites, Mexicans, Puerto Ricans. Young people and old, and they all looked at peace. I had never witnessed such a thing. There was ocean blue furniture, bright white walls, and fresh flowers everywhere. The instruments were polished to a shine and the smell was invigorating. This was not a service but an experience.

I looked toward the stage and saw my mother up there singing. I was in shock. Her eyes were watering and her face was glowing, and she beamed when she saw me. When I smiled back, I churned inside and thought, She's alive. She was beautiful, devilishly beautiful, and she had peace like the sun in her soul. After the songs, a man went on stage and grabbed the microphone and spoke to us.

"Happy Thanksgiving and welcome to Victory Outreach Ministry. Take your seat. You are going to hear some live testimonies from people that were once not people." I wondered what that meant. The first person that walked on stage was a slim black guy with a black hoodie and blue jeans. He grabbed the microphone and began talking.

"My name is Daryl Vasser and I grew up in the hard streets of Chicago. I soon realized that for many families, including my own, violence was a way of life. I can remember far back when I was five, I literally watched out the window as my stepfather beat a man beyond recognition because he owed him money. That was the beginning of me witnessing many more acts of violence, drug abuse, and drug dealing. By the time I reached twelve, I already began to experience and get involved in all these things as a result of adapting to this way of life.

"I believe the drugs had the most effect on me personally. I started smoking weed at thirteen, and by the age of nineteen I was already a drug addict and didn't even know it. It wasn't until four years after that when I found myself behind jail bars frequently that I realized I had a problem. I became very angry towards my family because it was right at home where I was introduced to drugs.

"My mom and stepfather sold weed, my big brother sold and used weed and cocaine, and of course, just as most twelve-year-olds who have a cool and popular big brother, I wanted to be just like him. Now that my life has been changed, we have forgiven each other. I have forgiven myself especially for the pain I have caused my mom in my addiction, and God has restored our relationship.

"This change came as a result of my mom praying for me. She started going to church and began to cry out to God for my life. Victory Outreach came to my neighborhood, I went into the home, and I've been clean ever since. I am not the man I used to be, and I know one day God will give me a family. Thank you."

Everyone clapped and shouted. Then my mother was next, and my heart started pounding. I felt a little embarrassed, hoping she didn't point me out. Very softly and slowly, her hands shaking, she said, "Hey, my name is Sister Linda Cooper. I am a mother of four and my kids are here today."

Everyone started clapping. She went on, "I want to thank God for my salvation, because I was supposed to be dead in some alley by now. I can't believe I didn't lose my mind from all the drugs. I mean, every drug you name, I done it and I was addicted to it."

She started crying and people shouted to encourage her. "Come on now, you got this!"

She continued, "I was all messed up, I was a cheater, and I stole from my kids. I didn't know how to love my kids. I was angry, I hated my life, and so I made a decision after I spent all my kids' money that I was going to kill myself. I mean, I was sitting there with rock cocaine in a TV antenna, smoking it. I couldn't look my kids in their eyes anymore. I was walking down the street with my head down on my way to end my life, and then a guy handed me a flyer and said 'Jesus loves you.' When I looked back, he was gone.

"I walked to this woman's house to call this place on the flyer. Her name was Ms. Stella. She was an old wise lady in the neighborhood who helped me out from time to time. We called the Victory Outreach program, and they said they were full. Ms. Stella wouldn't let me leave her house. She said, if you go back out there, don't ever speak to me again. I stayed there in bed for three days until I got a call from Victory Outreach. They said there was room.

"So I got up and left and walked and walked. It was so far, it had to be miles. I had no money, my feet was hurting, but I felt something pushing me towards the Victory Outreach home. I wanted to turn around, but I couldn't. Something was pushing me. Ever since that day, seven months ago, I been clean, I been changed, I have hope and a future, and there is no looking back."

I was clapping; I didn't cry, but I wanted to. At that moment, I decided to try and let it go, all the hatred I had towards her, the pain, the memories of kids at school making my life hell because of her addiction, the sleepless, hungry nights. I said, "God, if you're real, open my heart eyes to see that this is for real." In my heart, I had forgiven her before she opened her mouth. I didn't want to, because that year had seen my darkest hours and my deepest depression. But I knew when she came home I had to be patient with her, love her, laugh with her, talk with her, pray with her, walk with her, and try to get to know her.

After service, my mother sat with us and had dinner downstairs in the church fellowship hall. I couldn't stop staring at her because she looked so different. She even sounded different. We laughed and talked, and she told us about the people she was living with and the early morning prayers and songs that changed her life. She had nothing but great things to say about her director Carol and this Victory Outreach place.

I never believed in God because of my situation and my environment. I was always very confused about this God. Growing up, I saw people shot and killed, and I heard their families say there was no God if all their babies were dying. Then there were those who would get hit and survive, and say it was only God who spared their life. I was indeed confused. That day, I wondered what it was that saved my mother. I was interested to find out.

Hearing the testimonies, I learned that Victory Outreach was a Christian-based but non-denominational church that could be found in nearly every inner-city in the world. I heard the pastor say that their mission is to reach the drug addicts, the gang members, the prostitutes, and the broken-hearted. Even the "goody two-shoes" who have never broken a plate in their life.

"What we have in common is that we are suffering from a void," he said. "So we look for love in all the wrong places. We try money, drugs, sex, fame, parties, pills. And because of that we end up crying out for help. That's where Victory Outreach steps in. We offer a home for men and women. We have youth programs, church services, sports programs, workshops. See, we are not just some other program, some social agency, or some little church on the corner. Some of our people tried AA, tried a psychiatrist, doctors, gang programs, jail, and nothing worked. It wasn't religion but a spiritual relationship with God that changed us.

"It's like a big watermelon: I can take it and split it open and eat it and tell you it tastes good, it's so juicy, but until you try it yourself you will never know. God called us out of the ghettos to go back to the ghettos and make a difference. We are called to reach the treasures out of darkness, people that were once not people, but are now beautiful people of God."

It made some sense to me what this man was saying after seeing how my mom changed. Everything my mom learned from that church she brought back to our household. I didn't really mind it, as long as she didn't go back to drugs.

....

Now my brothers complain a lot and talk about moving out all the time. As I'm getting ready for school, I know it's going to be a long day. All I can think about is my brother Shaundell, and the feeling of sadness and anger is still upon me. Our family still has our issues. I am thankful that we are not where we used to be. We are not where we want to be, but my mom works every day to get us there.

We head our different ways to school. My younger brother Isaac and little sister Pamela are at the local junior high school, Shaundell is a junior at Farragut, and I attend Manley Career Academy. The year is 1997 and Manley must be one of the most violent high schools on the West Side of Chicago. I am aware that Manley graduates less than fifty percent of its senior class every year and only sends ten percent to college. What I do like about Manley is the five career preparation schools within the school, like a trade school. They are Medical Arts, Graphics & Technology, Construction, Business, and Foods & Hospitality, which I attend. I want to be a chef.

During 4th period, everyone is cooking omelets, while

I quietly work on a poem, trying not to think about home. As I'm writing my masterpiece, I hear footsteps behind me. Nisha—a tall, skinny, dark-skinned, very loud, and obnoxious girl—dumps a hand full of salt on top of my head and shouts, "Get up and cook, nigga." Without thinking, I jump up and force my forearm in her neck. She starts punching me on the top of my head. With my forearm pressure on her neck, I stop and stare in her eyes and ask what her problem is. I realize that I'm freaking out and let her go. I know, and she knows, that I am a kind kid, and not in a million years would I usually react like that. She is just being her normal, obnoxious self. I like Nisha; she is responsible for most of my laughs. Chef Singleton, our instructor, tells us both to take a seat and he doesn't report us to the office. Chef Singleton likes me a lot, and knows I have what it takes to be great, but he knows I'm always in my head.

We sit down and everyone is quiet. I can feel her looking at me with tears in her eyes, still in shock. I never look back up. I feel really bad—I've never done something like this before—but I know it is a result of how I felt last night. Some of the class is happy and thinks Nisha got what she deserved. I am ashamed; I go back to writing. I only have a couple sentences so far:

Sometimes I wonder, sometimes I think,
As I am lying in my bed, hopeless, will the sailboat really sink?
What I mean is, like the great big Titanic,
As the boat was sinking, people love to start to panic.
I don't have the looks or the charm or the smarts
But what I do have is a huge, pure, undivided heart.
I don't have skills that are recognizable by all,
To some, I am probably a shepherd boy, waiting on God's call.

I write this poem for the one and only Grace, the smartest girl in our sophomore class. She has light, caramel-colored skin, half-inch dimples, a perfectly round head, and neck-length, natural black hair. Plus, she looks so good in purple. Her eyes are brown and shine like a diamond. I love to hear her talk in the hallways. Her voice carries a southern lilt; it is sweet and she speaks only goodness. Her body isn't important to me, but she does have a heavenly body— she is a cheerleader. She is different from any girl I know, as if she was made whole. She seems easy like Sunday morning while the other girls seem hard to deal with like Monday morning.

Freshman year, she chose Derrick. Light-skinned, handsome, swagged out, tall, in-shape, basketball-playing Derrick. He is the perfect gentleman and an affable scholarathlete; he ranks number one in our class. If you made a movie of our class, Derrick and Grace are the ones you would make a couple. I have heard through the grapevine that they are broken up and she is not taking it well. This is good and bad news because for some reason I feel like I am the one that can open up her heart. It's been a long time coming, but the problem is we never speak. I don't even think she knows I exist.

The bell rings and it is lunch time. My pride won't allow me to apologize to Nisha. I am just glad to have favor with Chef Singleton. Walking into the lunch room, I see a long, skinny, white boat, and behind it a television monitor showing people racing in the same boat. I have never seen this before. I look closer at the TV and see nothing but white people. I lose interest and walk away. A white woman grabs my shoulders and asks me if I'd like to be on the rowing team. I tell her, "no, thanks," and walk to the snack station to buy a soda. In front of me is some pretty boy classmate asking to buy super donuts. When the lunch lady turns around to get the donuts, he steals chips and tosses them to his friends. When she turns around, he says, "It's okay, I don't have my money."

I sit down at a table with my homeboy Preston. We've been

in the same school since fifth grade. We know each other's families well. We are best friends. Preston is a tall, skinny kid with clear brown skin, tight eyes, and short hair with amazing waves. He is by far the smoothest and most confident kid I know, and the ladies love him. He is also a very curious person. It seems to me that Preston gets his swag from his mother, who is considered the coolest mom in our neighborhood. Her name is Michelle, and people say she has sold weed for the longest of anyone. I'm not sure and never judge because she plays no games when it comes to raising her children. She makes sure that her kids' grades are good, and if they're not, they are punished. Michelle always welcomes me in her home with open arms and feeds me when I have a bad family situation. I have never told her what's going on; she just knows, I guess. A mother always knows. That saying is true.

....

Preston and I did a lot of bad kid stuff together, like ringing door bells and setting off car alarms. Anything bad, we've done it. One time in sixth grade, Preston, our friend Jermaine, and I were walking down the street after smoking our first joint—which I hated—when a pimped out drop top car pulled up. It was Big Mike, one of the local neighborhood gangsters.

Preston said, "This is a nice ride."

Big said, "You guys want to get in?"

Preston said, "Hell yeah, let's go, Coop!"

My friend Jermaine told us not to get in the car, but I thought to myself that riding around with Big Mike would probably get us women and status. I told Jermaine I would see him later. He shook his head in disappointment. We rode a single block in style, but by the second block about ten police cars screeched in from every direction and surrounded us. They pulled out their guns and ran toward the car.

"Put your damn hands up!"

One cop said, "So you guys stole a car, huh?"

I didn't know what the hell was going on. Preston and I were screaming with our hands up. A cop yelled for me to shut up with a gun pointed at my forehead from a distance. Another cop told me I was going to jail and would get raped.

They pulled us out of the car and put Big Mike in one police car, and Preston and I in the other. We started crying in the back seat and people were walking past laughing. I wasn't sure if I pissed myself, my heartbeat stopped, or I got slapped in the face, but I was scared senseless. No doubt about it, I was terrified of the cops. I'm scared anytime there is a group that can smack you, search you, talk to you whatever way they want—or even shoot you—and get away with it. I figured they couldn't lock up themselves. I promised myself I would never be in a police car again. At the police station, Big Mike told the truth and we were set free.

"See what happens? This is the last time I'm smoking weed." To which Preston laughed and said this was also the last time we'd be getting in Big Mike's car.

....

Preston and I are such good friends that I know I can share almost anything with him. I tell him I had a bad night at home, without details, and he tells me it's all good and that I will get over it. I spend the whole day at school waiting for it to be over. Once school is over, I walk outside and see a crowd in the street of about ten guys walking towards someone. The lone guy is yelling, "Four Corner Hustlers!" At the front of the group is the same light-skinned pretty boy that was stealing in the lunch room.

I see him throw an orange at the one kid, and when the kid's hands go up to block it they all rush him. I see one of them hit him with a right cross, and he falls hard. The crowd is getting big. They start stomping him. One guy picks him up so that they can hit him some more, and I can see his blood flying with his spit. Girls are yelling out, "You killing him, you killing him!" And they drop him to the ground. They beat him until he's shaking and his eyes are rolling in the back of his head. Then a guy with a box haircut gets out of a car, pulls out a gun, and asks, "Do I need to use this?" The group says no and they all run.

These boys are called the Straight Off Albany Gang. They are the biggest gang in school. I witness the S.O.A.'s beat people into seizures more than once. I also see these guys take bags full of piss, tie them in a knot, and toss them into the crowd. No one will confront them. During separate days in the month of October, fifty or sixty of them throw eggs into the afterschool crowds. One day, all the security guards from the school are fed up, and fifteen of them start marching towards the gang with their white shirts on. It seems like the security guards are about to do some damage until one of the kids gives the signal and eggs come flying in from everywhere, hitting the guards until they run back into the school.

There is no stopping these guys; they do what they want, when they want. This isn't new to me at all. I feel like I've seen worse, even though it seems like my school is a war zone. It's actually a piece of cake compared to how I grew up.

....

Before Mom's change, my life growing up in Chicago went something like this:

9:00 a.m. - 2:30 p.m.:
I was at school most days, where the kids would clown me for being dirty and for being the son of a drug addict. Kids would fight all day long trying to be the hardest and to prove that the gang they repped was the toughest. The teachers spent most of their day yelling and breaking up fights, so

we didn't learn anything. Some kids felt pressure to choose which college they would attend; I was under the pressure of what gang I was going to join. I was asked about it almost every day. All my friends from school were Vice Lords, both of my brothers were Gangsta Disciples, and my uncle was the general of the New Breeds.

2:30 p.m. - 7:00 p.m.:

Every day after school, I was outside walking the streets of Chicago with friends I trusted, and some "friends" I didn't trust. When I say the ones I didn't trust, I mean the ones who were with me, but always clowned me and my family in front of everyone in school. Why I hung out with them, I don't know. On that walk, I would see my friends' parents buying drugs, and sometimes my own. They were all so skinny, roaming the streets like zombies, yelling and making weird noises to each other. I would see the older guys from the gang in nice cars driving around with loud music or beating the crap out of people. Some days, I would see those same guys in the back of police cars. There weren't many parks in our neighborhood, so we would just walk around or stand on the corner. We were easily bored, so my friends would come up with plans: steal candy from local grocery stores, steal bikes from Mexican neighborhoods, chase an innocent kid home, ring doorbells and run. We would also do a lot of what we saw the older guys do. When we saw the older guys from the hood smoke weed, we would take tree leaves, roll them in a piece of paper, and try to smoke it. When they beat the crap out of someone, we would go slap a random kid. When they talked about a night at the club and having sex with women, we would invite girls to our club house to touch on them. I thought it was cool on those streets, but at the same time I knew something was wrong. It was just that at that point, anything was better than being home.

7:00 p.m. until bedtime:

I was home by seven, but most of the time there was no one else there but my little sister and my grandmother. My brothers would run the streets until ten p.m. I would sit and watch television, waiting and hoping that my mom might scrape together enough money for food that night. That usually meant fried chicken, Spam, bologna, or sardines. Most nights I went hungry. It was always uncomfortable at home because in the winter there was no heat, and in the summer it was too hot and we didn't have air conditioning. The windows would be wide open and bugs would fly in, because there were no window screens. I remember all of us sleeping on the kitchen floor with the oven door open because it was so cold and we couldn't afford heat. Not to mention the roaches and rats who made themselves at home because of the lack of cleaning. I had to wash all my clothes in the kitchen sink by hand every night and pray that they would dry because if not, I would have to wear damp clothes to school. My brothers would finally come home and we often wound up fist fighting over something stupid. Around midnight, my mom would come strolling in drunk and high, crying with her usual scene.

That was every day of my early childhood, and I am glad it's over.

....

I rush home after school to see if Shaundell wants to shoot hoops or something, but as usual, he isn't home. My mother asks if I want to go pass out flyers with her in the neighborhood. When she graduated from Victory Outreach home, she developed a passion for telling everyone and their momma about the home, so I tell her I will go with her. She thinks I like it, but I don't. I'm a little embarrassed by the whole thing, but I'm always afraid of my mom running into old friends and going back to drugs. Plus, I made a promise to myself that Thanksgiving night she testified in church that I was going to walk with her.

When we walk the neighborhood and she sees a drug addict, she tells her story and they are touched and want to change their life too. My mom calls the home, and the van comes to pick them up. With my mom back, the neighborhood changes slowly but surely. I am proud of my mother. See, Christians believe that once you get saved, all things become new. God forgives, and you leave the past behind. What some Christians forget is that you also have to clean up your mess. Starting your life over again also means undoing all the damage you caused. I can see that my Mom is trying. She is restoring her relationship with her kids, giving back to those who helped her, and coming out with the truth, like what she did with my brother last night.

It's almost bedtime, and I am thinking about my grandfather. I know he was born in the forties in the south. I wonder what he saw that made him so angry and broken. Was he denied jobs because of his skin color? Did he see his friends get hanged? Was he beaten for just walking down the street? Was his family raped in front his eyes? How many times was he called nigger or wrongfully treated? All I know is my grandmother picked cotton. I don't want to make excuses for him, because I am sure that there are men who went through all the same things and yet still became strong fathers and role models. It hurts my brain to think about it, and I fall asleep.

When I get to the lunch room the next day, I notice the big white boats are still here. This time, the rowing people are saying, "Come to the gym room today to sign up and get free pizza." I figure that no one showed up yesterday.

I joke to Preston, "These people don't get it. Black people don't know how to swim, and you going to place them on a boat flying across a lake?"

"I was thinking maybe we should join."

I give Preston a look. "Hell no! I can't even swim."

"I can't swim either, but the lady said free pizza and we even go out of town."

"Nope."

"Come on, dude, let's just get pizza and leave."

I tell Preston I have an idea.

"After school, if you hook me up with Grace, I will go. I will even join the damn team."

He takes a deep breath and says, "I will hook you up with anyone else but her."

"No one else will do."

"I will introduce you two, then you take it from there."

I tell Preston he has to tell her I like her.

"Listen, I can't sleep. I am writing poems about this girl, and when I am having the absolute worst day of my life, the thought of her gives me peace."

Preston looks at me funny and gives in.

Preston knows Grace well because he dated her best friend for a while. He's also a smooth talker. I trust him when it comes to girls. He doesn't seem happy about the arrangement; maybe he feels like I am shooting for the stars.

As soon as school ends, I am excited and nervous at the same time. I have been rehearsing what I'm going to say in my head all day. Well, honestly, I've been rehearsing all year. Preston and I are waiting by the stairs at the main entrance for her to come down and walk out. Fifteen minutes pass, no Grace. Thirty minutes pass, no Grace.

Preston tries to talk me into still attending the rowing demonstration, but I'm going home. He tries to tell me we have a deal, but I tell him there is no deal if he doesn't introduce me to Grace.

"No Grace, no Rowing."

Preston can tell I am going to be stubborn, and decides

to go without me. I head home and start watching a scary movie with my brother Isaac. My mom comes in and asks if we've seen Shaundell. We shake our heads, not even looking up from the TV. Mom tells us that these movies are not allowed in the house.

"Why not, Mom?" Isaac asks.

"Because fear is not of God, and you're only watching for fear, to scare yourself. Why would you want to be scared? Be inspired."

I have no answer for that, so I tell her I will go read To Kill a Mockingbird for English class. I get through one page, close the book, and ask my mom if I can have ten dollars to go get a haircut. She gives it to me, and I head to the barbershop.

....

The barbershop is the black man's country club. That's where I went when I was bored. I figured it was better than hanging in the streets like I used to do. My mom made it very clear that if you hang in the streets, you have to go. The barbershop sold everything: gym shoes, T.D. Jakes' preaching tapes, porn, weed, candles. You name it, they had it.

The topics being discussed would range from R. Kelly to O. J. to, of course, the Chicago Bulls. It was funny listening to them. One day, a man talked to me about changing the world. He told me we have to change ourselves and change the way we think.

He said, "Listen to me, young man. I went to Europe, and while I was there I saw somebody from the West Side of Chicago. He was blown away to see me there. That man told me that this is really a small world, and I told him he was wrong. If you look at the map, it's huge! This is a big world we live in, but you and I can choose to expand." He told me to choose to expand. Dare to be different. To me, that was really deep.

I said, "Yes, sir."

....

When I get home, Shaundell is still not back, and my mom is calling everyone. My cousin tells her the guys he is hanging out with are in a gang war with another gang. Why he tells her that, I don't know. She is worried. She tells us that maybe we should all get on our knees and pray. I get on my knees and just think about Grace the whole time. I figure he will be home later.

My brother is a Gangster Disciple. He joined the gang a long time ago when my mom was still on drugs. Now that she's out of the recovery home, he is struggling between hanging with the guys and working on our new life as a family. I have my struggles too, but I always tell Shaundell that being out there is like dying for a neighborhood you don't even know. The homeboys tell you they got your back, but weeks later you're nothing but a memory. There is no way I am going to trade my life in for a spray-painted shirt, a forty-ounce, and a R.I.P. sign on the wall. I'm worth more, and I tell Shaundell he is too. He even mentions joining the Victory Outreach recovery home just to get away. He tells me he will join in his own time. I know that my time is now.

I wake up to my alarm clock and my mom singing her songs, and we are all a little annoyed. She says, "Let's pray for Shaundell. We still don't know where he is. Let's just pray that nothing happens to him. Let's all sing a song!"

My mom and I, along with Isaac and my little sister Pamela, start singing one of my favorite songs, "God Will Make A Way."

The song reminds me of when my mom first got out of the home. She would sing that song when there was no food in the house, or when she didn't know how she was going to pay rent. She would sing that song and BAM, there was a solution.

Old spirituals usually bring peace into our household.

I have all the faith in the world that my brother is coming home and he is okay. It's like a chair: when I go to sit down, I don't check the legs to make sure it's going to hold me up. I just sit down, and it holds me. It's the same with Shaundell. I am not going to call around asking his whereabouts because in my heart I know he is fine.

....

I see Preston in the hallway after second period, and he tells me I missed out because rowing was pretty cool. Apparently, they have some machines that are crazy. He also tells me Grace didn't show up downstairs yesterday because she was at the rowing tryouts.

"Fool, you lying!"

"Yeah, I'm lying, but they will be back in the gym today."

"One word: Grace."

"Chill out, I got you."

The bell rings and the day has finally ended. I meet Preston downstairs by the front entrance again. He is telling me how the people from the old neighborhood miss me and are always asking how I am doing. I look up and see Grace walking out the back entrance near the teacher's parking lot. I grab Preston.

"Dude, there she is, go get her!"

I follow behind him as the door closes behind her. He opens the door and calls out. I am nervous and shut the door behind him and start pacing back and forth in the hallway. Three minutes pass and I am freaking out and talking to myself. After what feels like a hundred years, Preston opens the door and shouts out to me.

"Coop, get out here."

"Who, me?"

He looks at me with irritation. "Yeah, you. Come on, dude." I walk outside and there she is, my dream. I am frozen, so I'm thankful that she speaks first.

"Hi."

"Hi, I'm Arshay."

"I'm Grace."

I say, "Yeah you are!" She laughs. I don't say anything else, I just look at her. There is nowhere in the world I want to be but right here, looking at her while she is looking back. I want to ask her to run away with me. There is an awkward moment, and Preston says he is taking off. Grace says she has to go too, and she looks up at me.

"Maybe you can walk me to the bus stop next week?" she asks.

"I like buses," I tell her, and she laughs.

"Okay, see you guys tomorrow."

"Have a good night, Miss Roberts." I grab Preston by the shoulders and shake him. "Thank you, my brotha!"

We run back into the school, and I am so excited to keep working on her poem. Preston heads to the gym for rowing, and I tell him I have to go to the office to call my mom and tell her I'm staying. When my mom answers, she tells me I can stay but she still hasn't heard from Shaundell. She called the school, and he hasn't been there either. I hear the worry in her voice.

"Mom, did you pray?"

"Yes."

"Well, then, he is fine."

"Amen."

....

I walk into the gym and see a bunch of students standing over a gray contraption. It's a workout machine that has the same exact motion as rowing a boat; I hear someone call it an ergometer. I see the pretty boy dude who threw the orange and jumped the kid going nuts on the erg machine, not knowing what the hell he's doing. The instructor has a look on his face that convinces me he doesn't know what he got himself into.

The instructor asks, "What's your name?"

"Alvin Ross."

The instructor tells Alvin to take it easy because the machine costs a lot of money. Alvin gets up off the machine in a huff.

"Yeah, whatever, I can pay for that."

A fit white lady by the name of Jessica stands up and asks us all to have a seat on the floor. There are about thirty people in the gym.

She tells us, "I want to introduce you to the sponsor behind this program, the man who made this possible, Ken Alpart."

I see a curly-haired Jewish guy walk up. This white guy has a hole in his t-shirt, run-down blue jeans, and jacked up tennis shoes. We give each other a side-eye. He starts talking and isn't the best public speaker, but what he says is loud and clear.

Ken tells us, "Crew is not for everyone."

A huge six-foot freshman by the name of Malcolm yells out, "You mean black people?"

Everyone starts to laugh and Ken smirks a little bit. Preston tells Malcolm to let the man talk. I can't remember any all-black rowing team, so maybe Malcolm is right.

Ken goes on, saying, "It's a thinking man's sport. It doesn't matter if you have natural athletic abilities, what you need is discipline, commitment, focus, and the ability to work well with others. Michael Jordan wouldn't be the MVP for rowing because, in a boat of four or eight, you will not notice one person but a team. One unit: everyone works as one. You will be noticed for your leadership outside the boat. You must be willing to work your butt off. This sport requires strong core balance, physical strength, flexibility, and cardiovascular endurance." Everyone is looking at him like he's speaking Greek, but Ken keeps going.

"I rowed in college at the University of Pennsylvania, and I think it's one of the most underrated and hardest sports around, if not the hardest. This is one of the oldest Olympic sports. There are no all-black crew teams. You will be the first. This is a very white sport, as you saw on the television. We are not just trying to give you the opportunity to row. We want to give you the opportunity to think outside the box, be young entrepreneurs, go to Ivy League colleges, and travel the U.S.

"Those who are serious will go to Philly on spring break and see what it is like to be a rower, a college student, and explore the city. I went to Flowers, Marshall, and many public schools in the area with this idea and they all rejected it, saying this sport wasn't for their students, that it would not work. Mrs. Flanagan said yes. So, if you do this with me, you will succeed. Hear that, you guys? You will succeed. Let's have a great year."

I look at Preston and tell him this seems too good to be true. I am pretty sure putting a group of black kids from our hood inside a boat to race white people is a set up for disaster. But I think about what the man told me at the barber shop. Maybe I can succeed like this man is telling us. In my heart, I believe in seizing the moment and that an opportunity is a gift, so I ask Preston where we sign up.

If there is one thing I know about myself, it is that I don't miss out on opportunities. People who don't jump on an opportunity in our community have a problem. I heard a minister say it's like locking a person in a grocery store for two weeks and telling them they can eat whatever they want. You come back two weeks later, open the door, and the person is lying there, dying of starvation. I would say that person is pretty stupid. The opportunity to eat was everywhere and they didn't take advantage of it. I believe that's how it is on the West Side, in our schools. There are many opportunities that come our way to advance our lives; they are everywhere around us. They don't fall into our laps, but they are right around the corner. Rowing programs, internships, college trips, career days, job fairs. We take it for granted. Or we let daily obstacles distract us from pursuing it. I have my share of obstacles. Sometimes you have to let your mind and belief help you overcome whatever is in your way. That's the only way to keep from giving up and missing out on something great.

There was at least one time that I threw in the towel. Lucky for me, Fate threw it right back.

....

I remember my eighth-grade luncheon was supposed to be the great ending to our William Penn Elementary School experience. Everyone was talking about what they were going to wear, who they were going to dance with, the awards they would receive, the food, even the bus ride. I was also excited and had a long list of girls I wanted to dance with.

When it came to that day, my grandmother had no money to buy me a suit or simple dress clothes. I had nothing to wear. I called my mom at the Victory Outreach home to ask her if anyone there had dress clothes for me. She said she would ask around and call right back. I sat and waited by the phone, feeling like my world was ending. The kids at school had been mean to me since the fourth grade. They criticized my family. They laughed at me and called me Dirt as a nickname. I was punched, tripped, and hit in the back of the head with snowballs.

It was depressing, but that last month everyone had been so nice to me and I had no idea what changed. I thought maybe it was because of my mom's prayers. Whatever it was, I didn't want to miss this luncheon. My mom called back a few minutes later and told me there was nothing available but that I should pray.

"Pray? I don't know how to pray. I need to go; I only have

two hours."

Mom said, "Sorry, but you have to pray."

I was angry at everyone. I went in the room and locked the door. I prayed, but nothing happened. An hour passed and my eighth-grade teacher Mrs. Smith called and told me everyone was on the bus, wondering where I was. I lied and told her I was sick and couldn't make it. She sounded like she didn't believe me but said, "Okay, we will miss you."

I hung up the phone and ran into my room. With all my power, I started pounding myself upside the head with a milk crate, saying, "There is no God." Then I stormed into the kitchen and told my grandmother that once I left this place I was never coming back. I told her I was tired of being treated like a bald-headed stepchild. I walked out the door and ran to Cermak Street.

Cermak is the street next to the viaduct that separated the Mexican neighborhood from the black neighborhood. I crossed the viaduct alone, not caring what happened to me. I wanted something to happen to me. I let go, gave up. I figured if the Mexicans didn't kill me, I would call my Uncle Vince and ask if I could sell drugs for him. I didn't think he really liked me anyways because I didn't join the gang like my cousin and brother. I thought that maybe I could prove that I'm not a punk.

Thoughts were passing through my head at a hundred miles an hour. I walked a couple miles to my Uncle Vince's neighborhood. I asked if I could ride around with him and his boys. I was in his back seat; the speakers in his trunk were so loud that they were pushing me around. He talked about all the females he banged while his boys laughed. You could tell they were all afraid of him.

As I was sitting there, I thought about a time when my Uncle Vince was shot three times when I was in third grade. My Grandma and Aunt Tina were sitting on the couch crying and rocking back and forth. My Grandma would say something like, "He's so loyal!" My Aunt would say, "No one can stop him." Then my grandma replied, "He makes beautiful children." This went back and forth while I sat on the floor and stared. You can tell they didn't think he was going to make it, but he survived. It happened again years later when Vince was shot up in his car.

I also thought about the time we were all sleeping at home, three o'clock in the morning. My Uncle Terry screamed, "Everyone get on the floor, now!"

I jumped up along with my brothers, sister, cousin, and Grandma. My heart was racing, and I couldn't see anything in that dark. Terry screamed for us to get to the kitchen and stay down. We asked him what was going on, and he told us my Uncle Vince was in a gang war and they were going after the family. I put my face to the floor as if I was dead, hoping it wasn't true, hoping it was just another episode from Terry, who tripped off the hard drugs every once in a while.

Sitting in the car with Vince that day, I kept thinking about the pain, heartache, and sleepless nights he had caused everyone. I told him to let me out, I was going to a friend's place. He did, and I walked home.

······································

Here in the gym, thinking back to that day in the car, I can't help but think that maybe Uncle Vince and I are still alive for a purpose. There have been numerous times I was walking down the street or playing basketball when shootings happened right in front of me. I cannot believe I've never been shot. I feel like I am fated to be alive walking the earth for some reason that's bigger than me. I guess maybe I have a reason to live and have a story to help me during those moments I want to give up. So when an opportunity comes my way, I always think, "This is it. This is why I'm still here." I even think maybe this private,

Ivy League, first-class sport was sent here for me, or I was sent here for it.

I look around the gym and see some students I know from the neighborhood. They are the kids of drug addicts, prostitutes, gang members, and drug dealers. The people that we will race are possibly sons of lawyers, doctors, professors, and salesmen. I picture us in a boat next to them, and say to myself, "This is going to be interesting."

PART 2
UNIVERSITY OF WISCONSIN

My armpits are sweaty, which usually only happens when I'm nervous. It's the first real day of rowing practice, and I keep saying to myself, Be strong, be confident, as I walk towards the gym.

When I was ten, my family moved to the 1600 block of Pulaski, and Mom sent me to the store alone. On my way back, I heard the sound of the ice cream truck and police sirens, like two funky mixtapes playing at the same time. I was kicking an Old English can down the street when I sensed someone behind me. I looked back, and there were two nappy-headed kids with buck teeth running towards me. I took off running, scared out of my mind as one called me a sissy. I was terrified when I realized I had run past my apartment. I had no options, so I closed my eyes, turned around, and ran towards them screaming. When I opened my eyes, I saw that they were now running away from me. They ran past my apartment, and I ran inside. I realized being confident and fearless gets you where you want to be.

I snap out of that memory and confidently walk into the gym room. There are over a dozen people present, including Ken, Coach Jessica, and Coach Victor. Practice is inside the small girls' basketball gymnasium. I look around and see all the boys wearing basketball shorts and t-shirts with cut sleeves. I look over at Alvin. Why isn't this dude outside beating on someone or stealing something? There is something about him that makes me feel uneasy. Before I figure it out,

Coach Victor starts practice.

"Okay, everyone hands up straight. Now reach down and touch your toes."

"Stretching is for homos," Malcolm, the six-foot freshman, yells out.

"What you say?" Coach Victor yells.

"Stretching is for hoes!" Malcolm yells back while everyone laughs.

Victor looks pissed off. "Okay, I'm going to talk to you guys about the importance of stretching and who it's for," he says as he looks at Malcolm.

I realize that Malcolm is a very outspoken person that says whatever the hell he wants. He is one of those guys that smacks food out of your hands and you do nothing about it because he so big. Coach Victor is a cool, young, good look-ing, African-American physical trainer. A lot of the guys say he is too much of a pretty boy, but it doesn't matter to me because he understands us and is so down to earth and smart.

After stretching, he says, "Okay, guys, run twenty laps around the gym while the coaches step outside to talk."

The guys yell out, "Twenty laps? Forget that!"

Coach Jessica chimes in, "Come on, guys, it's a small gym; you'll be finished in no time. You got this."

Everyone likes Coach Jessica. She is a really fit, white, female rower. She doesn't play games, and you can tell she is tough as nails. When she does the stretches with us, the guys can't keep their eyes off of her, especially Preston. I think he's in love. When the coaches step outside, Preston grabs a basketball and says, "Let's run a full court game." We are all down for it and start playing. Five minutes later, the coaches walk back in, screaming at us to get back to running.

"But, this is cardio," Preston pleads.

Ken laughs and tells him he has a point.

"Nope, get back to running," Coach Jessica tells us, and

that's exactly what we do.

After those twenty laps, we are ready to die. None of us are in shape. The coaches ask us to have a seat while Jessica demonstrates how to correctly use the rowing contraption called the "Erg machine." She sits down on it as Preston and a couple of the other guys drool and stare at her sky-blue pants.

She tells us that sitting on an erg is like sitting on the boat, and the boat is like being in a shell, a very narrow shell. She bends her knees and reaches for the handle while the seat slides forward. She reaches as far as she can, and her head is past her knees. She is so flexible. All the guys think it's pretty sexy, and I'm sure she can see us smiling. She tells us, "Now, guys, I am at the catch. When you row in a boat, you have the choice to start your race this way. When I say row, I am going to push back with my legs, then lean back with my body, and pull with my arms."

Jessica shouts, "Row," and drives back with smooth power. She is perfectly demonstrating how to use the machine. She tells us that if we hear the fan going, it's a sign that we are working.

"Okay, guys, grab a machine and let's row. Ken, Victor, and I will walk around and help you."

I get on the machine, and it feels good. The erg works your legs, core, arms, chest, and shoulders all at the same time. Ken walks over to me and shows me the correct way of rowing. I ask him if I will get this in a day, and he assures me I will. All the coaches gather around Malcolm. He is so big that his strokes are rocking the machine like he's on a boat, and all the coaches have to hold it down. We can tell the coaches are impressed by how strong he is.

After a few minutes of rowing, we complain that it's painful, but I can feel the muscles growing. We do ten minutes and are pretty beat and sweating up a storm. Coach Jessica tells us to take a five-minute water break, and we head out of the gym in a big group. We head down to the vending machines and head back into the gym room eating our snacks. The coaches start yelling.

"No, no, no!"

They come running towards us, and I jump and think maybe something is falling. Ken snatches the Flaming Hot Cheetos out of my hand, and the other coaches collect the grape and orange sodas from everyone else.

Ken tells us, "You just messed up your workout!"

"What? How?" I ask him, confused.

The guys are pretty pissed that they had the soda snatched out of their hands. I see Alvin ball his fist up like he is going to knock someone out, so I keep my eye on him. Ken tells us he wants to talk to us about nutrition. He explains the food chart, and talks a lot about the body and what it needs and doesn't need. I'm surprised when he tells us that fried food isn't healthy; I just know it tastes good. I can see that everyone is tuned in to what Ken is saying. We understand what Ken is telling us, but know it's going to be a hard road. I know the guys all want to look good, have a six pack, and live a long life, so we promise Ken that we'll try to eat better.

We get back on the machines and learn how to move in sync. The coaches show us how to move as a team and tell us how fast the boat will move if we work together. We have a pretty good practice, and I am excited to be a part of something new.

....

When I get home, my mom is sitting at the kitchen table. She points at the seat across from her and tells me to have a seat. Oh God, what now? She tells me that Shaundell called and said he is fine.

I jump up and yell, "I told you," and try to leave, but she tells me to sit back down.

"Arshay, he's moving out."

"Mom, you yourself said if we can't handle the rules then we have to leave."

"Yeah, but is it that hard?" she asks me.

"No, but no one wants to get up and sing songs every morning."

"But if it was the WGCI radio station you guys would be singing them in the morning as you get ready."

I laugh and agree.

My mom sits quietly for a minute and then gets up out of her chair.

"Listen, I know I messed up in my past, big time. But I am a different person now. We have dinner together. I work, I provide. Well, God provides. I am going to go down as a testimony. From the moment my eyes was open from my addiction, I done everything a mom was supposed to do according to God's word."

"You are, Mom. Look at Vince. He's a gang leader, but now he is working on getting out, going to church with us. Uncle Terry is at the Victory Outreach home in California and about to graduate. Aunt Jennifer stopped doing drugs the moment she witnessed your change and now she going to church. Aunt Tina, she's now getting involved in church. Your whole family, Mom."

She sits quietly, looking at me, weighing my words.

"It's all because of you, your prayers and spirituality. Religion couldn't do that! All I know is that I didn't believe in anything, but now I believe in something, and it lives in you. Mom, you always tell people, 'Train up a child in the way he should go, and they will never depart from it.'

"It doesn't mean we aren't going to make mistakes or want to move out, it means what we learn will always be inside of us. And when it's time to change, we won't need a book or an altar—we will already know what to do. You didn't teach us the way we should go, but you truly trained us, we living it!"

She replies the way she always does, "How did you turn out so good?"

I say what I always say back to her, "I was going to ask you the same."

•••••••••••••••••••••••••••••••••••••••

When I was in eighth grade, I missed about sixty days of school, which included a streak of nearly thirty consecutive days. When I decided to come back, a teacher stopped me in the hallway and looked me in the eye.

"You are going to die before you are eighteen years old, if that."

I looked at him and didn't say anything. I wanted to agree.

I believed it because Mrs. Smith, my eighth-grade teacher, always told us that statistics say that one out of three of us will die before we are twenty-one. I would look at my two best friends, Preston and Donald, and tell them, "Holy crap, that's going to be me."

Their family situation, their grades, and their luck were always better than mine. When that teacher said that to me in the hallway, I felt sick to my stomach and wanted to be gone for another month. I wanted him to know that my Mom was away at some rehab home. Or that some days I would go to the grocery store to help people carry their bags to make money to eat because my grandma couldn't support us all. I was tired of wearing the same clothes to school and didn't want to be here. He didn't ask, and he didn't want to know. No one asked; if they did, they only asked one time and never looked into it.

I never got good grades in junior high. How was I supposed to? How was I going to learn? I couldn't think about numbers when the only thing on my mind was if my mother was going to die in the streets. I couldn't focus on reading with a hungry stomach or learn about Christopher Columbus when my apartment was like World War II. I never learned about opening up or dealing with my feelings, so I kept everything inside and in my head, and it weighed me down.

So when this teacher looked at me that day as a bad, lazy kid and predicted my future, it made me depressed. But I also felt like I wanted to prove him wrong. I wanted to beat the odds. I didn't know how just yet, but I knew it started with just listening and doing the opposite of what my friends were doing. I think that's the start of being a good kid. As long as I did the opposite of my friends, I began to hear, "You're such a good kid."

And that felt good to hear.

••••••••••••••••••••••••••••••••

After talking to my Mom, I go to my room to work on my poem for Grace. I know I'll be walking her to the bus stop tomorrow. The goal isn't to give her the poem right away. I want to write it like a timeline, just keep writing as we get to know each other. I figure that's better and seems more thoughtful. I want to be more creative and to make it hard for her to resist. I also notice that my creative juices only flow on really good days—or really bad days—and today is a good day.

I jump up out of my bed like I'm having a nightmare. I am actually excited to go to school. There are only three things that make me excited to go to school: class trips, home basketball games against a rival, and when I'm going to see a girl. I'm not looking forward to my classes, just Grace.

Public school is tough, especially for teachers. In our classes, there are at least thirty students; sometimes one class has members of three or four separate gangs. Our teachers spend a lot of time breaking up fights. Good teachers are creative enough to keep us interested in our subjects so there is no room to think about the guy on the other side of the class-room. I realize that it's tough; some of these gangs are even separated from each other in prison. The teachers have to be peacemakers, mentors, parents, friends, security guards, and social workers. It's stressing them out; I notice it through their daily breakdowns.

I know the problem starts at home. These students have no rules at home, like I didn't before my Mom went to Victory Outreach, and it makes the teachers' lives hell. I believe when my Mom changed, my teachers' lives changed. She became a mother and built her home on God, family, and education. I caught on to it too, and it made life at school a little better because I was better. So I believe when the parents change, a teacher's life can change. I wish every kid had parents that knew about Victory Outreach.

···

I used to be one of those students that believed that teachers didn't have feelings, that it was just their job. My eighth-grade teacher, Mrs. Smith, sat us down one day to tell us her father died. She was in so much pain. She said, "Guys, I am going to take time off to bury my father. I ask that you guys pray for me, behave, and be nice to each other. I love you guys, and you are my family."

For the next week we had a substitute teacher and did what all kids do when they get a substitute teacher—we acted like savages and went buck wild. There were fights, we played spades, we ran the hallways. Security was in and out of our classroom.

The next week, when Mrs. Smith came back, she looked at us for five quiet minutes. I knew we were in trouble. She started crying and said, "I buried my father, my only father. I could have spent more time with him before he died, but I was here with you. I don't regret that, but I trusted you guys."

I saw that she was so hurt. Some of the students started crying. Mrs. Smith opened her heart and let us have it, but we saw how much she loved us. Then I saw something I had never seen. All the students started to lift their hands and say they were involved and that they're sorry. And right before I raised my hand, one of the girls said, "It was everyone except Arshay."

I was surprised because I had been a little crazy and because this girl used to laugh at me. All the other students agreed and told Mrs. Smith that I hadn't done anything. Mrs. Smith looked at me and thanked me. Then she looked back at the class and said, "You will all be punished. Payback is a motheryouknowwhat!"

I had no idea what happened there, but I realized how much hard work a teacher puts into us, and I wanted to do good by them from that day forward.

At Manley Career Academy, there were good teachers, but there were also some...not-so-good teachers. One time in history class, I asked my friend Deshaun how in the world he got a B grade in Math. I knew Deshaun didn't do school work or homework. He told me, "The teacher told me to keep doing well on the basketball team and he will keep passing me."

I told him I thought athletes were spoiled: that's why everyone wants to be one.

He laughed and said, "Don't hate."

"More power to you."

I learned the lesson that not every educator is a good teacher.

....

School went by so fast today. It's already my last period, and I can't concentrate on what I am going to say to Grace while I walk her to the bus stop. Everything I think of seems lame. After thinking too much, I decide I will freestyle. The bell rings, and I walk downstairs to wait for her. A couple minutes later, I can hear her saying goodbye to the security guards, teachers, students, and anyone she walks by. Heaven must be like this. She sees me, and we lock eyes and smile.

"Hey, how was class?" she asks.

"Better than yesterday."

She laughs. She always laughs.

She asks, "Shall we?" I take the book bag from her arms.

I can tell she seems impressed, as if no boy has done that before. I'm happy I thought of it. We start walking down Polk Street towards Kedzie, and I ask her about her classes and the cheerleading team. It is all about her, and I am happy to let her talk. It's like listening to my favorite song. I walk slowly because we are only walking two blocks.

When we get to the next street, a car with five guys inside pulls up. In the driver seat is the guy with the box haircut who pulled out a gun that day the SOA gang jumped that kid. He yells out, "Grace, come here, let me holla at you."

"No, I'm good."

"Come on, you got a boyfriend or what?"

"I'm good."

I am debating whether or not I should say something. I'm walking a very thin line. On one hand, I'm thinking that I need to be a man and be hard and show Grace I'm not a punk. On the other, I'm being strategic. If Grace is a smart girl, she understands that these guys are trouble. It could go either way. I know these guys want trouble, they want me to say something.

To my relief, she says, "Don't mind them. That is so disrespectful."

Thankfully, they drive away, and I'm relieved. I feel the need to get out of the hood, and I'm willing to do whatever it takes to leave, but the hood is all I know.

•••••••••••••••••••••••••••••••••••••••

We get to the bus stop and wait, and I'm praying silently that the bus won't come. I talk to her about the rowing team and the speech that Ken Alpart gave us. She thinks it's cool and tells me I should stick with it. I see her bus coming so I tell her I wrote her something.

"Let's see it."

I tell her it's not finished and won't be for a while.

"Okay, I can't wait to read it." She hugs me and steps onto the bus.

"Tomorrow?" I ask her, and she looks back and smiles.

"Tomorrow."

I run back to school for rowing practice, practically floating. When I get to the gym, I tell Preston what happened.

"Did you get a number?"

"No. Why? I am going to see her in school tomorrow."

"Man, get that number and try to hit that!" I laugh and tell him to chill out because I know what I'm doing. Then I get an idea.

"We should take Grace and her friend Lisa on a double date."

Alvin walks up. "Lisa who?"

I turn around and look at him, in shock that he heard us. I know he is a troublemaker and don't want anything to do with him.

"Nobody."

"I heard you, homie. Lisa who?"

Preston tells him, "light skin Lisa."

Alvin asks if Preston is messing around with her, because he is too. I'm nervous because I'm sure there's about to be trouble. Preston just laughs and says yeah and then they're shaking hands and talking about how cute she is.

I tell Alvin, "You know you guys could have killed that kid."

"Keep that on the low, dude. He beat up one of our friends."

I decide it isn't my business and start warming up on the erg.

Coach Jessica tells us to stick around after practice so she can talk to us about a special trip. We are all extra pumped for practice and anxious to find out where we're going. We fly through our normal routine of laps, strength training, and rowing machine drills; all of it fuels my nervous energy. After training, Coach Jessica tells us what we're dying to know: there will be a team trip next Saturday to the University of Wisconsin.

"They have what we call a rowing tank, an indoor facility which attempts to mimic the conditions rowers face on open water. Once you use this, you will have an idea of what it's like to row."

....

We pull up to the University of Wisconsin on a Saturday. I notice everyone here looks so happy; they smile and wave at us. I've only ever seen this on TV, and never in a million years did I think I would experience it.

The coaches begin talking to us about what college is like and how we would have the best years of our life if we decide to go. Malcolm asks Coach Victor who paid for us to come here, and Victor says, "Ken. So thank him when you see him."

Malcolm says, "This school is cool, but way too many white people."

Preston tells him he's a black racist.

"No, I'm a black realist." I just laugh at them both. They stay on each other's case.

We walk into the athletic facility and are amazed. As we check out the place, some of us start wrestling on the mat. Malcolm is slamming everyone, so I tell him I will wrestle him. Everyone starts rooting for me. The coaches consider me the hardest worker on the team by now, so even they stop to look. As soon as I grab Malcolm he slams me right on my back, and everyone starts laughing. Without a doubt, he is the strongest and scariest guy on the team. I get up and tell him he's strong, but not so tough.

"We'll prove it on the next erg race."

"Okay, whatever," he shrugs.

We head down to the rowing tank, so excited that we hop in it right away. There are about nine guys on this trip, all of us serious, since Alvin didn't make the trip, which I don't mind at all. As I'm sitting in the tank, I realize it really does feel like a boat.

Coach Jessica says, "Okay, guys, grab your oar. An oar is used to move the boat. Oars are long poles with one flat end that is called the blade or spoon. The spoon of the oars is normally painted with the colors of the club to which it belongs. It identifies boats at a distance."

"So ours would be red and black," I tell her.

"Yep, that's a great combo," she replies. "There are two types of rowing. There is sculling, which requires two oars per person, and there is sweep, which has one oar per rower. We will be rowing in a sweep. Now, each rower is referred to as a port or a starboard, depending on which side of the boat the rower's oar extends to.

"If your oar is to your left, you are a starboard, and if the oar is to your right, you are a port. You can row in pairs, fours, or eights. The goal is to have an eight person team and a four person team. Rowers have other titles and roles. In an eight plus boat, the stern pair is responsible for setting the stroke rate for the rhythm of the boat to follow. They lead. The middle four are usually the less technical, but more powerful in the crew. The bow pair is the more technical and set up the balance of the boat. Lastly, you have the coxswain."

Preston interrupts her mid-speech, "The cock's what?" Everyone starts laughing and Coach Jessica tells him his mind is always in the gutter.

"The coxswain is the person who usually sits in the stern of the boat, facing the bow, and coordinates the power and rhythm of the rowers. This must be a lightweight person."

She tells us she wants the stern pair to come up the catch. "You guys learn this in the gym on the erg machine. It's the same motion, but you just have an oar."

She gives us the signal, and we start rowing. She adds on the next two rowers, and the two after that, until we are all working in sync. It's a beautiful experience. We can't wait to get on the water one day. We get a tactile feel for what it is like to row. I see everyone's faces and start to believe this might actually work.

"Way enough," she yells, which means to stop rowing. You can tell that everyone feels good to be a part of something and we're all happy to be out of the neighborhood.

Walking back to the car, I tell Coach Victor that have I always wanted to travel without being in the Army or Navy.

"You will have plenty opportunities, being on the first all-black row team."

"We're in the late nineties: I can't believe that first black anything still exists."

"Tell me about it," he laughs.

On our way home, Preston asks if I want to hang with him on the West Side in the old neighborhood for a little bit.

"No, that's not me anymore. There is nothing over there for me."

"Your old friends, they always ask about you. Don't forget where you come from."

"I don't forget," I tell him, "that's why I don't go back."

"I want it to be like old times, when all of us just kicked it on the porch doing nothing."

"I get it, but I don't wanna be in the wrong place at the wrong time. And there won't be a wrong time if I can avoid the wrong place. I won't be hanging out on the corner or some porch no more, and that's just the way it is."

He shakes his head slowly and tells me it's all good. I just look at my feet.

....

I spend my down time with some of the older guys from the Victory Outreach home. I am intrigued by their stories, and they're funny. Whenever we're together, they talk about leadership and change. It's a little weird hanging with all these ex-junkies, but I notice they enjoy my presence as much as I enjoy theirs.

When I get dropped off at home, I see a man walking around with his shirt off through the front window. I can't tell who it is. When I get inside, I see that it's my stepfather, Ike. I haven't seen him in years. Ike is the father of Isaac and Pamela, but he helped raise me whenever he wasn't in jail. He is tall and muscular, with a huge cut going down his stomach. He has dark skin and a deep voice. He's wearing Dickies cargo pants, and I know he just got out of jail. I shake his hand.

"Hey, 'sup, man?"

"Just got out and happy to be home."

"Really?" I ask him. "I thought jail was home."

"Come on, man, I am trying to change," he tells me.

I tell him that trying isn't good enough.

"Well, I'm going to church with you guys Sunday."

I tell him that's good, and that it's good to see him, and walk into the bedroom I share with Isaac. My Mom and Pamela share the front room, so I can't figure out where Ike is going to sleep.

He yells after me that he wants to catch up and hear about my grades.

"For sure," I yell back, slamming the door.

....

When I was a kid, I spent a lot of time with Ike while Shaundell spent time with my grandfather. Ike would take me to the grocery store with him and try to teach me how to hustle. "When a person comes out with a cart, don't ask to help carry the bags, just grab it and say 'Where is your car?' If they give you less than a dollar you say, 'What's this?'"

He was always telling me, "You have to hustle to make it in this world." He never once taught me anything about love, reading, loyalty, math, or faith. He only talked about survival, plain old survival.

Ike once asked Shaundell and me if we wanted to play outside. He had us stand on the corner and dribble the basketball and play there.

"And if you see a police car, scream, 'Hey, mama!'"

It sounded easy enough, so we obliged, not knowing we were part of his street team while he sold drugs on the block.

There were times I was in the car with him and he would stop in the middle of the street. He'd walk over to other cars and tell them we'd run out of gas and ask them to help us. "My son is just sitting in the car, scared," he'd tell them while I just sat in the car, confused.

I didn't understand my purpose for being on this earth, but I knew that this was my life, and I didn't complain to anyone about it. I kept everything inside.

I knew I cared for this man when I was about ten years old. I was sitting on the couch and my mother was in the front room, screaming at Ike through the door. He was in the hallway, pleading, "Why would you leave me? I love you!"

"Leave me alone," she screamed back. "It's over. I will call the police if you don't leave."

"If you don't open this door, I will kill myself. I am not playing around."

"That's your business, but I want nothing to do with you, Ike."

Ike got louder. "I'm going to kill myself. I can't live without you, Linda."

My mom didn't say anything. Ike told me through the door that if I didn't open it, he really would kill himself. I sat there quietly waiting until my Mom turned her head, then ran quickly to the door to try to open it. I got as far as the knob, and my Mom grabbed my arm and threw me across the room as she yelled at me. I remember hitting my head on the wall and hearing Ike say, "Linda...your son!" Everything went dark and got smaller, and then I blacked out.

When I opened my eyes, I heard my Mom screaming and saw Ike standing there with his stomach cut open. I could see his insides hanging out.

My Mom was screaming, "Oh my God, he did it! He did it!" I backed up to the wall with my head on my knees and closed my eyes. I blocked out the noise, the smell, everything...and imagined falling, because when you do that, there is nothing to think about but falling. That day put a hole in my heart that I didn't know how to fix.

Ike had his issues, but there were good memories too. He would let me sit on his lap while he was driving, showing me what to do. I remember him bringing food home. He would stop my Mom from hitting us with extension or telephone cords when she would beat us until our skin ripped open.

....

Even though I think of Ike as my step dad, I can't figure out if I want him around. I know he's the one who introduced my mom to drugs, and now that he's here I'm afraid of her going back.

Ike shares prison stories with us while we eat dinner at home: me, Ike, Mom, Isaac, and Pamela. I wish Shaundell was here too, but he's out doing his thing. Some of Ike's stories are funny and some are violent. It reminds me that prison is a

place I don't want to end up. Ike tells us that he learned a lot
and went to church in prison. Everything seems okay, at least
for tonight, but I still plan to keep my eye on him. After we
finish dinner, I head outside to chat with Ike while he smokes
a cigarette. He tells me, "I'm still tripping off your mother. She
is a changed woman that loves going to church! Who would
have ever thought?"

"I know," I reply.

"You know I'm a Christian, right? I went to chapel every
day," he says proudly.

"Yeah? Well, I hope you know going to chapel every day
don't make you a Christian just like sleeping in a garage every
day don't make you a car."

He laughs and tells me he's trying.

"Don't try," I say.

"I know, DO."

I tell Ike that everyone from the family is off drugs and
going to church now. Then I tell him one of my favorite stories
that my youth leader told at Victory Outreach.

"There was a little boy who took a long walk in the streets
of Chicago. On his walk, he saw a mother and her child sitting
on the ground with a sign that read, 'Hungry Please Give.' He
saw gang members jumping a little innocent boy into a gang.
He saw a mother and a father trying to trade in their food
stamps for cash so they could get their drug fix.

"He saw a hooker getting smacked around by her pimp
with nowhere for her to run. He saw people leaving a funeral
that was the result of gang violence, while a broken-hearted
family wept. He saw a young girl with a mini-skirt hanging
around with guys, looking for love in all the wrong places. He
saw two brothers wearing backpacks get bullied by the local
school kids while others stood by and laughed.

"He saw posters of missing kids on telephone poles, and
young boys no more than thirteen in the back of police cars

with their heads hanging down. Right there, he developed a burden and began to question God. As a tear rolled down his face, he said, 'God, if you are up there and if you are real, do you see all this madness? Do you see these hurting people, their pain, their tears? If you do, why don't you do something about this?' And God replied, 'I have already done something...I made you.'"

Ike smiles and nods his head. "I love that."

"My mom was real crazy out in the street, but now that she's saved she's like that little boy. She believes she's here to change the world, and so is the person who gave her that flyer. It's bigger than going to chapel, Ike. It's about what you do outside of chapel."

Ike tells me I'm a good kid and have always been his favorite. It feels good to talk to him like this.

We take the bus to church together, and when we arrive the greeters are very happy to see us. They talk to Ike before service starts, and I can tell that he feels comfortable. During praise and worship, I see Ike lift his hands. I'm shocked and can't stop staring.

When the preacher comes forth to speak, Ike gets up and tells us he is going to the restroom. The service goes on, but Ike doesn't come back. After a long time, one of the ushers comes to our row and asks my mom to step out for second. I get nervous, wondering what could have happened. After a few minutes, she comes back to our seats and I give her a questioning look.

"Ike went to the coat rack and stole all the leather jackets."

My little brother Isaac laughs and says, "I knew it!"

I tell him to shut up. "You okay, Mom?"

"I'm not, but God is in control."

I guess my conversation with Ike didn't go too far. I was trying to get him to understand that it's not just trying or wanting to change. I believe you have to make a choice; you have to decide. When I was ready to stop acting like a foolish kid, I made a choice right there and then that I was done, and after that, I never went back.

....

I head down the stairs at school to meet Grace so I can walk her to the bus stop. When I see her, I tell her my good news, "I was chosen to compete in the cooking competition at Washburn Culinary School."

"That's awesome," she says and gives me a hug. "What do you have to cook?"

"I have to do a knife skill test and cook four different egg dishes, some without using a spatula. Everything has to be perfect."

"I'm happy for you."

"Well, thank you," I say with a smile on my face. Being around Grace makes me want to succeed.

"Arshay, I have a name for you," Grace says. I tell her I want to hear it.

"Molotti."

"Ooookay," I say with a confused look.

"Molotti, Molotti, more head than body!"

I laugh. "You got jokes. You know you have a big head too."

"I know, but yours is bigger!"

"Fine, Molotti it is."

As we walk, I debate in my head about asking her on a date. The walks are good, and I'm getting to know her. I know what makes her smile and what makes her sad. I know her favorite food, her favorite person, and her insecurities. I study her and listen to every word that comes out of her mouth. I want to make sure that I don't get thrown into the friend zone. I know she has a wall up: I see countless guys try to talk to her, and she waves them off. I made sure to take my time to get to know her, to give her inspiration, stories, laughs, trust, friendship, and to share my dreams. I have no doubt in my mind that this is the right thing to do, but I have it bad for this girl, and I want her to know.

Knowing it's probably time to make a move, I tell Grace I have a question. She asks me what's up.

"I want to take you out for dinner or a movie, like on a date."

She takes a deep breath. "I want to, but I'm still in love with Derrick, and it's not fair to let you take me on a date when I still love someone else."

My heart feels like it's coming out of my chest, it's beating so hard. I don't know what to say.

"I'm getting over it," Grace says. "Be patient with me."

"If there is anything I've learned over the years, it's patience," I tell her.

I just want to get to rowing practice at this point, so I tell her I'm late for practice and we can catch up tomorrow. She whispers, "Don't be mad at me, Arshay."

I assure her I'm not, and just need to get to practice.

"Okay, Molotti. Come to my place for dinner this week. I want you to meet my family."

I agree, knowing I must look like a sad puppy, and she says she will call me later.

Walking back to practice, I think hard about the bomb Grace just dropped on me. I figure that Grace needs a shoulder, an ear, a friend. Every guy around her wants something from her since she's so smart, pretty, and sexy. So the best thing I can give her is my shoulder and inspiration. I still can't shake my ego, which tells me to forget her and not to let her use me as a shoulder. Here I am, walking that thin line again, and I know I can be blown in either direction. I think about a scripture my Mom always repeats: "Don't grow weary in doing good, for you should reap if you don't give up." I've watched enough Wonder Years, Family Matters, and Saved by the Bell to know not everyone gets the girl right away.

When I get to practice Coach Jessica tells me I'm late again, so I tell her I had cooking stuff to do. She tells all of us to listen up because she has some big announcements.

"This week, everyone will take a swim test, and we will get in the boat for the first time."

We start clapping and screaming. She tells us that the coaches need to test us before choosing who is going to Philadelphia for spring break. I've noticed for the last week or so how the numbers on the team have grown since the coaches started advertising the free Philadelphia trip. Coach Jessica says she also wants us all to choose Team Captains today.

"Shouldn't we know if our captains can swim first?" Malcolm asks.

Before Coach can respond, I say, "Arthur and Elliot." The gym goes quiet. "They are the two most mature guys. They don't clown around."

Coach Jessica asks if everyone is okay with that and they all are—except Malcolm, but majority rules. I don't think anyone has earned being a Captain yet, but if they are going to give it, Arthur and Elliot are great choices. I learned at Victory Outreach that leadership is not the position, but the action you put in.

Arthur is a strong and sturdy senior with a reserved personality. He is a man of few words, but when he talks, people listen. Elliot is a junior and kind of a loner. I always see people teasing and making fun of him because he has a Jheri Curl perm and a box haircut. The jokes are mostly innocent but he is a nice guy, and I feel bad for him. We've bonded because we both want to be chefs.

We head to the YMCA to learn how to swim; it's a funny scene. There are about fifteen boys and four girls. Coach Jessica and Coach Victor tell us that the ones who know how to swim should go first so they can see what we can do. Alvin jumps in the deep end and swims like a fish. I'm surprised that he can do anything besides beat the living crap out of someone.

The girls all say they know how to swim but don't want to get their hair wet, and we laugh. Malcolm says, "You hoes don't know how to swim." Coach Jessica shouts at Malcolm along with the girls. It seems like no one on the team really cares much for Malcolm.

The coaches realize no one knows how to swim besides Alvin and Elliot, so they start working with us one on one. Alvin helps the coaches out by teaching some of the guys. Everyone is goofing off and throwing each other in the pool every time a coach turns their back. After Coach Victor shows me how to move my arms, he asks me to swim from one end to the other. I start off at four feet, and as I pass five, six, and seven feet, people are clapping and cheering me on. I pass eight, and when I get to nine, I freak out and start to go under. The lifeguard jumps in and pushes me over to the edge. Everyone is laughing like crazy so I smile as if I'm fine, but I am terrified. Most of us are. Coach Jessica and Coach Victor are looking at each other like they need a raise. In the locker room, the boys are slapping each other with towels and goofing off. I'm sitting quietly because I'm so embarrassed. Preston picks up a towel from the bench.

"Whose towel is this?"

They let him know it's Elliot's, so he uses it to dry off in-between his legs.

Malcolm's eyes go wide. "I can't believe you butt flossed with the man's towel!"

Some of the guys laugh when Elliot comes in and about to dry his face with the towel. When he looks around confused, I tell him Preston used it to dry off, and Elliot storms out of the locker room.

One of the teachers that helped show us how to swim walks into the locker room a few minutes later. He's a short, nerdy white guy. He says the room smells like uncircumcised penis and asks us what's wrong with Elliot. Malcolm tells him that Preston butt flossed with his towel, and he winces.

"Eww, that's a bad one."

....

I rush home from swim practice and quickly change to go to Grace's for dinner. When I arrive on the twenty-first block of Springfield, it's one of the scariest corners I've ever seen…and I've seen scary. There are kids everywhere selling drugs, and they're all staring at me like I'm a three-legged monkey. I'm a little nervous because I know you can't just be a stranger walking into a neighborhood, chilling with girls from their block. That's a no-no. Also, taking the bus over is an even bigger problem, but I don't have a car.

She lives on a dead-end street next to the viaduct. I say to myself, I must love this girl, because I am going to die. But when I get to the door and knock, she opens it with a warm smile and invites me in.

She introduces me to her mother, Karen, and her two little brothers. Right away, I start playing with her little brother and his toy cars. I love kids, and he is the cutest thing. I talk to Karen about my classes and brag about how I think her daughter is the smartest girl in school. Grace and I both live in a single parent home and we both understand what it's like. After dinner, Grace asks me if I have something for her.

"No, why?"

"What about the letter?"

I tell her it's going to be a long time before she gets that, I'm still working on it. I feel like as long as I am still working on it, she is with me always. I want to kiss her right there in her room but I know I have to respect her wishes. It's like having cake in your hand and someone reminding you you're on a diet. It's making me a little crazy. I have to understand that Derrick was her first and only, and it takes time to get over that. It also seems like Derrick isn't giving her a straight answer about how he feels, so I guess the waiting game continues.

I know she thinks she's being strong by holding onto him, but as my aunt says, you are stronger if you can let go. I want Grace to know what she's worth, and I promise her I will be patient with her in this process.

Two hours pass. As I'm leaving her place, I say, "Wish me luck walking to the bus."

She laughs. "It's not so bad over here."

"You wear glasses."

I kiss her on the forehead, thank her mother, and leave.

....

After school on Friday, we jump in a van and head to the Lincoln Park Lagoon for our first day of rowing on the water. We are nervous to go, and when we pull up we see the boat-house. After all our practicing, it is still amazing to actually touch a boat and pick up an oar, and I can't believe we're here.

Ken meets us down at the boathouse, and everyone is happy to see him. Some of the guys secretly call him the Cool Cracker. He is always telling us jokes and giving us words of inspiration, and you can tell his love for young people comes naturally.

Coach Jessica tells us it's time to pick up the boat and goes over all the different parts. She explains everything we need to learn to use, from the seats to the strapped-in shoes to the oar locks. It's a lot to remember. She walks us through on how to successfully take the boat off the boat rack to the water. "Stand in front of it and reach over with one arm." We grab it, slowly pick it up, and pull it out, and every other person goes under while the others keep holding on so we have the boat at our waist. Then we lift the boat to our shoulders—four on one side and four on the other—and carry the boat to the dock, carefully. When we get to the edge of the lagoon, we lift the boat over our heads, grab the inside, and slowly place the boat into the water. The process is simple but still nerve-racking.

A few of us head back to get the oars while a couple guys stay and hold the boat near the dock so it won't float away. We are shown how to put the oars in the oar lock, and then it's finally time for us to get in the boat.

We are all a bit shaky.

"This boat is so skinny. How in the hell are we gonna get in here?" someone asks. Coach Victor assures us we'll fit, and Elliot asks if we have to put our feet in the shoes and get locked in.

"What if the boat flips over?"

Coach Jessica says we should trust her that the boat won't flip, but Malcolm blurts out, "Forget that," and walks back up to the boathouse. The coaches yell after him to get back down here, and ask where he's going.

"To get a life jacket," he yells back. All our heads pop up.

A mad rush for life jackets begins and the coaches are imploring us to return to the boat. Ken convinces the coaches to let everyone get life jackets if it makes them more comfortable. Elliot, Alvin, and I are the only ones who don't get one. It wasn't that I was confident in my swimming ability, but I wanted to stand out.

When it's time to get in the boat, I chide the others. "It's a shame that you guys live on blocks where there are stabbings, robberies, and drive-by shootings every day and yet you're scared to get in the water."

Malcolm asks why I'm not scared.

"I am. I'm also scared of shootings, but I still go outside."

"You think you so clever, Arshay," says Danny, a gang member from another neighborhood. I get the feeling he doesn't like me. I figure he is on the team just to go to Philly.

We get in the eight-seat boat in pairs. Each person climbs

in with visible uneasiness, slowly putting their feet in the shoes, not wanting to strap in. I don't think it has ever taken this long to get any group on a boat. Once we're finally all in, Coach Jessica jumps in the cox seat, and we feel a little safer with her onboard. Alvin and I are in the front of the boat: the bow pair. Preston and Malcolm are the stern pair. Preston asks Coach Jessica how much the boat costs, in case we ruin it.

"About thirty thousand dollars," she says.

"Daaamn," says every kid on that boat.

Ken grabs an oar and pushes the boat off, wishing us luck. Deshaun squeals, but just like that, we are out in the water. It's is a little choppy and already Deshaun is close to crying, saying he wants to go back. Coach Jessica tells him to relax and instructs Alvin and me to row first, but we tell her we can't because we are afraid. Everyone is complaining; some are at the point of tears. To our relief, Ken tells Coach Jessica to bring it back in. I am just thankful that no other teams are on the water to witness all of this.

When we get off the boat, everyone is laughing at Deshaun. He doesn't care at all, he is still freaked out. The coaches look a little disappointed, but I don't know what they were expecting. This whole rowing sport is completely foreign to us. I want to tell Ken not to give up on us because we've been through a lot tougher, and we will manage this with time. Instead, I keep my thoughts to myself, and we put the boat away and walk to the van as if we just lost a race.

I realize that at least now I have a good reason to call Grace tonight, and I'm at peace.

PART 3
UNIVERSITY OF PENNSYLVANIA

I'm in the kitchen with my mom, helping her cook dinner. I tell her I want something healthy and explain the food chart to her the way that Ken explained it to us. We decide to make baked chicken and boiled vegetables, but my little brother and sister are unhappy with the menu. Pamela gets sent to her room for cursing because she wants fried chicken instead. She tries my mom's patience almost every day. Since my mom's big change, she doesn't hit us anymore. If she gets close to hitting us, they'll say something like, "Go ahead and beat us, be who you used to be." That stops her in her tracks.

Pamela's always had a dirty mouth, which my mom tried to put a stop to before she went into the home by washing her mouth out with soap every time she cursed. It was painful to watch. She knows my mom won't do that now, so she takes advantage. Although my mom doesn't hit us, she will put us on something called 'discipline,' a punishment she learned in the recovery home. It includes things like scrubbing walls with a towel, washing a neighbor's car, or cleaning our siblings' shoes with a toothbrush. I can't stand discipline, but it does reduce the fighting in our home.

I take the chicken out of the oven and walk to the front room for some air. As I get close to the door, I hear the knob start to turn and freak out, rushing towards it to hold it shut, thinking that it's the drug addict zombies. Before I get to the door, it pushes open, and I pray silently that it's Shaundell. The door swings open wider, and I see that it's not my brother, but Ken Alpart. I block him from coming in, my heart still pounding.

"What's up, Arshay?" Ken asks casually. He is with the female athletic director from the school, Coach Jones.

"Dude, you can't just be walking in black folks' houses! What's wrong with you?"

"I have to meet all the parents before the Philadelphia trip," he replies, looking confused.

"Hold on, I'll ask my mom to come out to the door," I tell him, shaking my head. We never have company, and I don't want Ken to see that we live in a one-bedroom apartment. I yell for my mom to come to the door.

"Mom, this is Coach Ken."

She looks at me. "The boat thing?"

"Yes, Mom, the rowing team."

I haven't told my mom about Philadelphia yet; I planned to wait until the last minute to inform her. I head into the kitchen to finish cooking the vegetables while my mom talks to Ken and Coach Jones. After they finish talking, I say good-bye and my mom closes the door behind them.

"Why didn't you tell me about Philly?"

I laugh. "I didn't want you to come up with any bright ideas, like I can go but I'll have to join the church choir or something."

She smiles. "That coach of yours seems like a really nice guy."

"He is one of a kind."

"It seems like it's going to be an experience."

"Yeah, if we can learn not to be afraid of water."

We both laugh, and she tells me that when I graduated from the eighth grade, she saw a vision.

"I have never had one like this before, Arshay. You will be great, and you will go places that no one in this community would ever think to go. You will be in the presence of kings."

I am blown away when she tells me this, but part of me also thinks she's trippin'. I know there's something special about her visions, because the people at church call her the Prayer Warrior. But when it comes to her predicting my future, I'm not so sure.

I tell my mom that out of all the coaches, we like Ken the best, so I'm excited to see what he can do with all of us. Ken Alpart is a thirty-two-year-old options and futures trader. He started his own company, Alpart Trading, in downtown Chicago and became a very rich man. I have heard some of the coaches say he is a math genius. He's also the founder of Urban Options, a foundation that works with kids on Chicago's West Side. Ken is dedicated to giving his time, talent, and treasure to local little league teams, hockey teams, and now the crew team. Ken also taught a youth entrepreneurship class once a week on the West Side. He's married to Jennifer Bonjean, a law school student, and they have a beautiful little girl named Winnifred. From the moment he stepped foot in our gym at Manley I knew that he meant business.

....

After school the next day, I tell the team how Ken just opened my door and tried to walk in my apartment.

"Hell yeah, man," Alvin tells us, "this dude knocked on my door too. I answered and told him to wait a second; I'm going to get my dad. I walked to the kitchen, and my dad had a look on his face like he's going to kill someone. I turned around, and Ken is right behind me. My dad doesn't play like that man. He don't even like white people."

Preston says, "My sister was yelling that the police were at the door!"

It seems like everyone has a similar story. I'm surprised he didn't get himself killed, but it's pretty funny hearing everyone's unique story of Ken just walking into our homes without permission.

"You guys don't call him the Cool Cracker for nothing," I tell the team, and everyone starts laughing.

A few days later, my mom says to me, "Remember how you said that I may come up with a bright idea before you go to Philly."

I eye her suspiciously.

"I want you to go to the Victory Outreach street rally with me tonight."

"Really, Mom?"

"Yes, I want you to come."

I know my mom spends a lot of time on the streets late at night with a group called the Twilight Treasures. They are a group from Victory Outreach that visits areas with heavy prostitution traffic and tries to get those women to go into the home. Some do and change their lives. Some last for only a week or so. Sometimes their families will join the church because they are so grateful for the change. That's how Victory Outreach grows.

I have never witnessed a church like this before. When these men and women complete the program, they get jobs, education, and oftentimes their spouse and kids back. I've also seen some come to the home, do well for a few months, and leave the home only to go back to drugs or gangs.

My mom always says, "You have to be sick and tired of being sick and tired. You have to want it for yourself, your kids, and your family."

I am really thankful for Victory Outreach. If not for Sonny Arguinzoni, an ex-junkie from New York who turned his life around and started this ministry, I don't know where my mom would be.

By the time my mom and I head to the street rally, it has already gotten dark. The mission of Victory Outreach is to offer hope in the places no one else will go. Tonight it is being held in the middle of the Robert Taylor Homes, a public housing project with dirty brick buildings and garbage strewn everywhere. It looks like a scene from New Jack City. I know I have to watch my back, but the Victory Outreach band, along with about forty others, have set up all their instruments and hooked them up to loudspeakers. There is a banner in front of the band that reads, "Stop the Violence."

They start with a song called "The Ghetto." After they finish, the guy I heard testify at the Thanksgiving service, Daryl, grabs the microphone and starts rapping to the group.

"It's not by power and not by might, but it's by my spirit, says the Lord!"

The rest of the group starts shouting, and soon people from the projects come outside to see what all the noise is about. Faces appear in every direction; people and their kids open the windows wide to listen. Between every rap and song, a couple people testify about how they used to be, how God came into their life, and what they are doing now. This is a radical ministry; I know that these are the same people who reached my mom over a year ago.

After ten minutes, there are numerous people standing in front of the band: gang members, drug dealers, prostitutes, drug addicts, kids, families, cops. Some are crying. Young people from the church get on the microphone and testify as does my mom and others. I think it's funny to watch the drug addicts out here, dancing and hugging each other.

Towards the end of the rally, the band sings a song called "Street People." It's a song about poverty, loneliness, love, and hope. While they play, I start to cry. When the song is finished the pastor of Victory Outreach Chicago, Pastor Fernando, grabs the microphone while the band plays softly in the background.

"Listen, we are not here to entertain you. We're not here to preach religion to you or to preach fairytales. We are here to let you know that there is hope, my friends. See, at one time, I was all messed up too. I was messed up because I liked getting loaded. I liked getting loaded so much that I ended up in jail. I liked getting loaded so much that I ended up in the hospital. I liked getting loaded so much that I started disrespecting my family.

"More than fifteen years ago, I walked into the Victory Outreach and I've never been the same. I'm a new man; God changed my life and he can do the same for you. Don't wait until you're behind bars to change, don't wait until they take your kids away to change, don't wait until a bullet hits you to change. There may not be a tomorrow…the time is now."

People are sobbing. I see the same gang members, drug dealers, prostitutes, and drug addicts asking for prayers and information about the home and church. People are hanging out the window with their hands outreached and some even run downstairs. One kid comes up to me and asks, "What about you?"

I'm caught off guard. I look around for someone else to help him, but everyone is talking to somebody. I sit with him and tell him about my mom and my life, and he tells me he has gone through the same things. I give him a flyer and tell him to give it to his mother.

"It will also change your life one day."

My mom tells me that this is what she does every week in the worst neighborhoods.

"And when you go through what I went through, you don't want anyone else to experience the same thing."

Victory Outreach is full of folks that want to spend their lives mending broken people and removing pain. I think about my teammates on the rowing team and wonder if they are going through some of the same stuff that I used to go through. I figure time will tell as I get to know them. I'm inspired to do something big, but don't know what or how.

I just know I need to keep training hard and listen to my coaches and mom.

....

There are a few days left of school before spring break, and everyone is pretty excited. I've been feeling a little impatient and plan to ask Grace what's going on with us before my trip to Philly during spring break. There's another girl, Tiffany, who lives on my block and has an active crush on me. I don't know why, but a year ago I told Tiffany I didn't want to date her, have sex with her, or even dream about her. I said I just wanted to play cards, laugh, and debate as friends. I was a little firm, but she hung in there until I matured.

I can't give Tiffany my heart right now because it's still with Grace. Which must be the same thing that's happening with Grace and me. She is interested in me but still waiting on an answer from Derrick, I guess. I always tell myself how dumb it is to wait on someone like this, but I'm still young and willing to put in the time. If I'm going to do that, at least it's with the smartest girl in our class and no one else.

When Grace and I are walking to the bus stop later, I decide to confront her.

"Are you done with Derrick? I need to know because I really like you. I love our friendship, but I like you." I should've stopped talking, but I continued, "There is kind of this girl that likes me—,"

"It's okay. I don't expect you to wait. You should try to make it happen with that girl." My body goes numb and my hearing goes out for a second. I am pretty sure I just died and came back.

"No, but I'm not really into her. I am just saying…"

"I'll tell you what; I will give you an answer for sure after spring break."

"Deal."

I will never understand why the ones we like don't like us back, or why we're never interested in the ones that actually do like us.

Listening to my mom's scripture readings, I've learned how love is supposed to be: gentle, kind, not boastful, not jealous, not irritable, not self-seeking, not easily angered. It keeps no record of wrong, never gives up, always protects, always trusts, and is always hopeful. I know that I need to practice having patience, especially when it comes to Grace. Patience has shown me some of Grace's strengths, strong aspects of her personality that I probably wouldn't have seen if I was actually with her. I've also seen her weaknesses, and patience gave me the opportunity to know what I can or cannot deal with before investing more time. I am starting to realize that if you don't take the time to get to know a person first, you will only waste time, and it may lead to an unplanned baby, a divorce, or a painful breakup. All things considered, waiting on Grace seems like the best step.

....

I am buzzing with excitement as I walk to school from the Blue Line train. It's a beautiful Saturday, and finally time for the team to go to Philadelphia. In the school parking lot, I see a huge white bus with "$7000" written on the window. You can tell it's an old yellow school bus that someone painted white; they did a horrible job. Ken is there with Coach Jessica and Coach Victor as the other students arrive. I ask Ken if he's driving with us, and he tells me he isn't but to make sure we behave.

When I get on the bus, Malcolm is sitting in the back next to a skinny kid with glasses.

"Hey, Malcolm, who is this guy? I never saw him before."

"This is my nephew, Pookie. He's visiting from Germany."

"He's your nephew?" I ask him. "He's your age."

"He's my sister's son, fool."

I laugh and nod at Pookie, and he shakes my hand and nods. I think Pookie is a little weird, or maybe just shy.

When I walk off the bus to say hello to everyone, I see a very short Puerto Rican woman. She has a mole on the right side of her face, baggy blue jeans, and a black leather jacket. She tells me in a thick accent that she's Mona Lisa, the bus driver. I want to laugh because she popped up out of nowhere and she's swinging a big Jheri curl in my face. I say hello back just as Alvin pulls up with his father, a tall, dark, and scary-looking man. He reminds me of the cook from A Different World. Alvin's brother, who is known as Pooh Nigga, is a senior at Manley and coming with us as well.

Once all nineteen students have arrived—fifteen boys and four girls—Ken asks everyone to get on the bus. Everyone kisses their families goodbye.

"Okay," Ken looks out over all of us, "I want you guys to have fun. I only have three rules: no baby making, no fighting, and listen to your coaches."

"Got it," we say back.

"Have fun, and see you there."

Coach Victor tells us to raise our hand when he says our name. "Arshay, Malcolm, Anthony, Preston, Leslie, Leah, Terry, Antwon, Tavares, Deshaun, Ronald, Alvin, Arthur, Tracy, Tanika, Joseph, Pheodus, Elliot, Danny."

We are all accounted for. I guess Pooh Nigga's real name is Tavares.

"Okay, guys, this is our training camp. Let's see who can make it past this, and then we're on our way to history!" We start clapping and shouting. I'm not sure if this is going to be a disaster or a success, but time will tell.

I do feel a little uneasy because I hate school buses. I've heard kids tell stories about getting their butt beat on the bus with no one to break it up because the driver is driving and doesn't feel he gets paid enough to babysit. The driver always looks like Leroy-from-down-the-block and they never have experience with kids. I've seen kids get bullied, teased, molested by older kids, and slapped around on the bus. You would think there would be a bus mentor present at all times, but I guess it's hard enough to even get kids to school in the first place.

Having Coach Victor and Coach Jessica on the bus with us is making me feel better about the ride.

The trip to Philadelphia has been quiet because no one really knows each other and this group has a few different cliques. About halfway to Philly, everyone starts complaining about their backs hurting because of the hard seats. It is pretty painful; I don't think school bus seats are meant to be sat on for more than a few hours. Coach Victor tells us to stop complaining since none of us are paying for anything.

About eight hours into the trip, we start singing songs and creating chants. A few of the guys get bored and put Vaseline up the noses of the guys that are asleep. They wake up angry, but no one will tell who did it. Other than that, the ride is pretty smooth. At one point, I head to the back of the bus to talk to Uncle Malcolm and Pookie. I ask him what it's like to live in Germany. He said it's okay, but in a low weird voice. I'm intrigued because I've never met anyone who lived in another country. He tells me that his dad is in the army and his mom is a nurse. I ask him about a thousand more questions, and I can tell he is getting a little annoyed.

Finally, he says, "Dude, I live in Chicago. I don't live in no damn Germany. I just wanted to go to Philly with Malcolm."

I just back up and put my hands up, "My bad."

"It's all good, but Malcolm is my uncle." I walk away, telling him to enjoy the trip.

....

We arrive in Philadelphia in the middle of the night, pulling up slowly to a large house in the middle of the woods.

As everyone wakes up, Malcolm shouts, "See! I knew they is going to kill us niggas out here."

Preston yells at him to shut up, but sounds nervous. Coach Victor and Jessica tell us we are here, and to get our things together.

We get off the bus and walk into the most beautiful house I have ever seen. It is the size of a mini museum and stars blanket the sky. Ken greets us all at the door and introduces us to his friends Ted and Tracy, who own the house. They are a lovely white couple with big smiles, and you can see their huge hearts beaming from their faces. They shake everyone's hand and show us around. Before we could put our bags down, everyone starts running around claiming rooms. Ken tells us he wants us all to get some rest,

"It's late, and tomorrow we are going sightseeing and Monday we will get right to work."

Ken goes into Ted and Tracy's room, and they shut the door. We go into rooms in groups of four; Preston, Malcolm, and Pookie are in a room with me. Malcolm tells us that something isn't right that Ken is in the room with Ted and his wife.

"What's not right, Malcolm? They're friends," I tell him.

Malcolm is lying down staring at the ceiling,

"White people be on some freaky stuff."

We laugh, and Malcolm says he's going to listen at the door. "Y'all coming?"

"No, go have fun," the rest of us tell him. He leaves the room.

I ask Pookie what's wrong with his uncle, and Pookie tells me he's been trying to figure him out for years.

I talk myself to sleep. I wake up an hour later to laughing and feel shaving cream on my face and a teddy bear in my arms.

"Real nice, guys."

Now that I'm awake, I go into the other rooms. There are another half-dozen people asleep with shaving cream on their face. I know right away that it's Malcolm and Preston. When I see Preston he tells me he wants to throw Alvin's shoes in the woods because his feet smell,

"No man, that's going to be a fight," I tell him.

"He won't know it's us."

"Because, it's not going to be us."

"Whateva." He grabs Alvin's shoes and tosses them into the tree line. It's going to be a long week.

....

The next morning there is fruit, bagels, and cream cheese on the table. Everyone begins complaining, asking where the donuts and cereal are. Ken has another talk with us again about nutrition. I go into the kitchen and check out the stove. It is stainless steel and I am in love with it. Ken walks in and sees me eyeing the hardware.

"You like that?"

"Yep."

"How is cooking class?"

"I got 92 out of 100 in a competition they had at Washburn College, but there were a lot better scores."

"That's good. Just keep working at it," Ken tells me, opening the refrigerator. "The nights we are at home I would love for you to be in charge of cooking. Are you okay with that?"

"I'm okay with that. I'm just grateful to be here."

He tells me to put together a grocery list and he will go to the store for me later. I feel honored to cook for everyone and to show what I've learned in the last year.

When I go back in the dining room, Alvin is asking everyone about their shoes and no one knows why. After a few minutes I can tell he is getting heated, so I tell him his shoes are in the woods. Preston glares at me.

"How'd they get there?"

"I'm not sure, but when I went for a walk this morning I saw some there. They may or may not be yours, but I will take you to them."

As we walk through the woods, Alvin talks about one of the girls on the trip. I tell him she is with a guy on this trip.

"Man, I don't care," Alvin says, "He is the size of my pinky. I'll smash that dude."

"Yeah, but if you smash him you'll be kicked off the team."

Alvin reaches down and grabs his shoes.

"Yeah, I just wanted to go to Philly anyway."

"Alright dude, you call it," I tell him, and we head back.

···

We spend the whole day checking out sights like Independence National Historic Park and the Liberty Bell. Preston asks if we can run up the Rocky stairs. Ken says we will, later in the week. When we get back to the house after sightseeing, Ken and the coaches explain the next few days to us. We are all nervous but excited to get out into the water.

I barbecue some chicken and pork chops for dinner, and it's a huge success. I notice Arthur's sister Leah has her eye on me. She recently joined the team, and I think she likes that I can cook a good meal, but I don't need another girl in my life. She is thin, light-skinned, and pretty with full lips. She has long braids that go down to her back. I tell Preston that Leah has been watching me.

"You must have a thing for Roses," he laughs.

"That's what I said!"

I feel like there is no room in my heart for another girl, though I don't think there's anything wrong with flirting.

Later, Leah does come up to me. We talk about cooking, and she asks how I learned to cook so well. We stand outside talking for at least an hour. I notice Arthur walking back and forth, checking us out. She tells me not to worry,

"He's my step brother, and I date his best friend."

"I'm not worried. We're just talking."

"Just talking?" she asks, looking me right in my eyes.

I laugh and stand up. "Girls are crazy."

"You're really mature. I like that."

"Hey, when you grow up the way I did you become a man early. If you don't, you pretty much stay a boy."

"Like Malcolm?" she asks.

"Like Malcolm."

We both laugh. It seems like everyone has issues with Malcolm, but I do like him. I think he is funny and a strong asset to the team, and he has incredible street smarts.

I head into the front room where Alvin is playing cards with his brother, Terry, Danny, and Elliot. They are playing Deuces Wild for dollar bills. Everyone is pissed because they have lost most of their money to either Alvin or Pooh Nigga. They seem to be very good at playing cards, and they tell us they've been playing that game for years. I notice that everyone seems to be getting to know each other better, but there are still some cliques in the group.

In the morning, we rise quickly and head to the University of Pennsylvania cafeteria. I can't believe it when I find out it's all you can eat. We're blown away by the beautiful college girls, so we split up and sit next to them. They can tell we are high school students, even though we try to say we are in college. We have seconds and thirds for breakfast, and I am in love with college. It reminds me of the television show A Different World. Watching that show inspired me to think about college for the first time, and now I'm getting the opportunity to live it.

After breakfast, we take the Marshmallow Man (our white school bus) over to the Penn boathouse. Malcolm tells us that

Mona Lisa has been drinking liquor out of her coffee cup.

"Shut up, Malcolm," we say in unison.

The boathouse is a beautiful brown, red, and blue field house with the smell of hard work and water. There are boats everywhere, and they are being polished like brand new Ferraris.

"Okay, guys, this is where I rowed," Ken tells us. "This is home to me. Respect everyone you see and let's work hard and have a good workout. Now go upstairs to the locker room and get changed."

We are amazed by the pictures on the wall, the workout room, and the crew shirts we see. The boathouse is full of tradition. I am so pumped and ready to go. Ken warms us up by taking us to go run the hills across the street from the boathouse. Terry, the most overweight of our teammates, is all the way in back for the entire run. He is yelling that he can't do it, so Ken goes and stands by his side, motivating him and pushing him the whole time. Ken talks to Terry about believing in himself and tells him that by the end of the week he will not be last. Ken asks a few of us to continue to push Terry, even though we are pretty exhausted. Some of us have never run hills before, and we're still out of shape.

When we get back to the boathouse, it's time to row. I feel like we're all so embarrassed from the last time we rowed that we are ready to erase that memory. Some of the guys are still making fun of Deshaun for crying on the boat. He says it's a conspiracy. Coach Jessica reminds us how to carry the boat. Some of the guys complain that the others aren't really holding their weight. When we get to the water, we lift the boat over our heads and grab inside, then slowly place the boat into the water. This time is much smoother.

After testing out our erg machine skills, they pick the best eight to be the first to row: Malcolm, Preston, Arthur, Elliot, Antwon, Ronald, Alvin, and I.

"That's some bull," Pooh Nigga says, "I don't want to be on the scrub team."

Coach Jessica calms him down, "You're not a scrub. Some of these guys will be on that boat too. Ken will do some work-outs with you guys while we row."

We get on the boat again in twos and push off. Calling the shots from a small motor boat and a bullhorn is Mike O'Gorman, a former Penn crew team member, employee of Alpart Trading, and the man behind this idea of us rowing. He's there to help with the coaching for a few days. Mike has won numerous national championships as a coach and also won medals in world championships as a coxswain. He's a short white guy with big curly hair that tells a lot of jokes that we don't understand, but he certainly cracks himself up. He remembers all of our names right away. From the bullhorn he says, "Bow two," which is me and Alvin, "I want you to go forward all the way up to the catch. When I say row, I want you to drive the blade into the water and row just like you did in the tank and on the erg."

Mike signals and we reach all the way forward. Our blade is sticking out of the water and pointing skyward while the other team members' blades rest on the water.

"Okay, make sure you row in sync. Alvin, follow Arshay. Ready…set…row!"

It's all moving so fast, but we drop our oars in the water, push off, and we are rowing! I can't believe I am in open water rowing in the city of brotherly love. We are talking over each other while trying to figure out how to sync our oars.

"Okay, in two rows I will say 'way enough' and I want you to stop and rest your blades in the water," Mike says, and we do it without any mistakes. He does the same technique with all the other pairs in the boat. He is a great teacher; he easily explains everything using different metaphors.

"Okay, now the stern pair," Mike says to Preston and

Malcolm, "seat seven and eight. I want you guys to go up to the catch. The stern pair is responsible for setting the rhythm for the rest of the boat to follow. When I say 'row' I want you to row and slowly the other pairs will join in."

We're all shouting that we aren't ready for that, but Mike wants to try anyway. Alvin whispers from the back,

"This cracker is trying to kill us out here," and I start laughing.

"Ready… set… row!" Mike screams, and we start rowing again, "Okay, in two, seat five and six join in. You guys are called the stern four. One, two, go!"

The other guys join in a little late, and the boat begins jerking. We start screaming every curse word in the book. The timing is off. Mike screams 'way enough' and he tells us we're going to start over, so we start again. He asks that this time we follow his voice.

"Stern pair to the catch, now row. In two, seat five and six," he shouts, "One, two, and row!"

They start rowing and the boat is gliding. It is a great feeling, and you can tell that we are all giddy. After several tries, seat three and four join in, and we are really zooming.

Mike has us try adding in the last two seats, but I don't go at the right time. The boat starts listing again. We see a team row past us giggling and hear one guy say "They have life jackets on." Coach Jessica, who is in the coxswain seat, tells us not to mind them, they're jerks. Mike tells us the good news is that we are really strong and just need to work on our technique. We see another team pass. They look so smooth, rowing past us so peacefully. I notice that their blades come out of the water facing upward, turn parallel to the water coming back towards the catch, and then drop back in the water facing upward. It looks effortlessly fluid. We ask Coach Jessica what that's called, and why we aren't doing it. She says it's called "feathering." She says that in a feathered position, the oar blade meets with less wind resistance. Less wind resistance means a faster stroke.

"You guys will learn that soon, now it's not important."

I am happy to wait. We spend an hour rowing and working on our technique and then pull into the dock. Four other students get into the boat. Coach Jessica keeps Alvin, Preston, Malcolm, and I on the boat; I'm excited because I am eager to learn more.

After our day of rowing, Ken tells us to go into the boathouse to shower. When we run upstairs, we see that it's a community-style shower. After some complaining about having to shower together and some corny jokes from Mike O'Gorman, we get on the Marshmallow Man heading for a Penn campus tour. We talk about our rowing experience on the bus the whole time. We agree that it is one of the hardest things we've ever done.

"To get eight guys to do the same exact thing, all at one time, and at such a fast pace with every part of your body is insane," Arthur says.

I sit up on my seat. "Agreed. You play basketball, you can play soccer, play baseball, hell, even sometimes play fight, but you can't play rowing, it's brutal. We can dance, run, throw, shoot, fight, kick, but rowing is foreign for us."

Coach Victor tells us that the odds are against us.

"But I'm telling you guys, we are really on to something here. I don't think there has ever been another crew of eight black men that have done this all together before, so you may very well be the first."

....

When we arrive at the campus, there is a huge rally going on. People are passing out flyers for various causes. Alvin asks for the team video camera and starts going up to people, asking about their thoughts on the possibility of a black rowing team.

Some people laugh, some people say it would be awesome, and some think that people would never take it serious.

Everyone walking around Penn campus seems to be cool, serious, and smart. It is a different world here, and I'm falling in love with the college campus. After walking around a while, we go into the W. E. B. Du Bois College House. Most of the programs and events in the Du Bois House are based on the history and culture of the people of the African Diaspora. There are five black students there to show us around, give us some history, and talk to us about college life as an African-American at Penn.

Towards the end of the day, we have a group discussion about gender, diversity, and education. This starts some pretty heated debates between Malcolm and Leah. I'm happy to learn about the diversity and power we could have if everyone came together. Although W. E. B. Du Bois is an African American-themed college house, it is one of the most diverse spots on campus. The students help us realize how important high school is if we want to get accepted to a good college.

On the way home I sit next to Alvin on the Marshmallow Man. I saw him really listening and tuned into what to our student guides were talking about, so I ask him why he's in the gangs.

"I'm not a gang member. I grew up with those guys. It's a rule if someone from your hood gets jumped, you help them. If not, you get jumped." He keeps his head down as he talks. "I feel bad for every guy we beat up. That's not really me. But if I want to be protected, I have to help. We go to a school with too many gangs. Who is going to help you if you get jumped?"

"I guess…Preston?"

"Yeah, but that's it."

"I understand where you coming from, but it doesn't have to be that way," I tell Alvin, "If I am walking on campus today and you bump me, at that second I am in control of the situation, not you. I have the choice to react like a hard, tough dude from the West Side or a smart young black man that knows that I'm responsible for my actions. Whatever I do decides the outcome."

He looks at me sideways. "You some kind of preacher or something?"

"No," I laugh, "but I've learned a lot from the youth service and the guys at my mom's church. You should come sometime. It's not a robe wearing, people screaming, money asking kind of church."

"Most people at church are phony."

"Most people on this bus are phony, and our school and homes. We still go there."

"Right, but did you know I never get into a fight because of me? Every fight I've been in is because of my brother, my sister, or my friends. I don't like trouble, it just follows me."

"It follows me too, Alvin, but I can run, and I'm fast as hell." We both start laughing, and I ask Alvin why his brother is called Pooh Nigga.

"He is really just Pooh, but it sounded too soft so we put the 'Nigga' behind it."

I nod, laughing, and tell him I have one more question.

"How do you and Pooh Nigga win the card games?"

"Don't say anything, but we cheat. We just let each other know what we get."

"That's cold," I tell him, and now we're both laughing.

When we get back to Ted and Tracy's house, Ken urges us to shower and tells us he's taking us somewhere cool for dinner. We get dressed and back on the bus as fast as possible. We pull up to another big house in the middle of the woods and find out it's a house owned by one of Coach Jessica's friends. They are hosting a party for us. Inside is a big table full of food, a party room that looks like a casino, and some very happy country folks. We feel welcome right away.

Ken tells us to turn on some hip-hop, and we run to the stereo to find tunes.

"Ken, what you know about this music?" says Joseph as he takes his girlfriend to the dance floor. Joseph is tall and slim of build, which is good for rowing, but I don't think he is into it long term. He's focusing on graduating, and that's all he talks about. He dates Leah's best friend, a sophomore. We figure he only came on the trip to keep an eye on her.

We have a great time and dance all night. When it's time to go, we can't leave because Mona Lisa is passed out drunk. Hours pass, and we chill and watch movies until she is sobered up.

We're scared on our way home because it's so dark, but Mona Lisa has it under control. I'm sure she's been in this situation many times before.

The rest of the week is strictly training every day. Our morning routine is breakfast on campus, running hills, two hours of boat time, school visit, and back to practice on the erg machines. Ken is usually the cool one that we love, but when it comes to training he is very serious. He pushes all of us way past our limits, even though we complain most of the time. He is really into helping Terry, and I notice he's shed a couple pounds. With the help of Mike O'Gorman, we learn to row together. It took a few days, but eventually we caught on. It is a tough week. Moving that boat with all of our strength for more than one minute requires us to be in top shape, but when we finally get it we feel incredible. We still see the other rowers looking at us as if we are flying dogs, but we know that it's new to their eyes and will take some getting used to. The life jackets aren't helping, either.

On the last day of practice, we walk over to the Philadelphia Museum of Art to the Rocky Stairs that we've been waiting for all week. We run up while chanting the theme song and dance around like we're Rocky Balboa. It is such a beautiful experience. I don't think I could have ever dreamt this.

When we arrive at Ted and Tracy's place, their whole family is there along with a few friends. They've laid out endless plates of food and want to get to know us better. Ken and I come up with an idea to have a talent show for the team and their family and friends. Half of the team signs up, and I am elected to MC the show. The first place prize is twenty dollars, second place is ten, and third place is five. The lights go off, and I feel like Mark Curry hosting Showtime at the Apollo. I am super animated, and everyone is laughing and having a great time.

Alvin sings R. Kelly. Terry does standup comedy and everyone boos. Pooh Nigga and Leslie do an African dance, Preston raps, and Ronald sings a song about marriage that has everyone crying and lands him in first place. Pooh Nigga and Leslie win second, and Terry wins third for effort. I ask if I can do a poem I wrote called "AM I" and Ken says, "Let's hear it." My heart starts pounding with everyone looking at me. I can't believe I'm doing this. I've written a few poems, but never read them to anyone but my wall. I take a deep breath and close my eyes.

AM I JUST SKIN THAT'S BROWN OR BLACK?
AM I BORN FROM LOVE, LUST, OR CRACK?
AM I MADE OF GOLD, SILVER, OR BRONZE?
AM I SAM COOKE RIVER ON THE RUN?
AM I A DANGEROUS BIRDY THAT'S BREAKING THE NEST?
AM I A LOCAL HERO WITHOUT AN S ON HIS CHEST?
AM I A STEREOTYPE THAT RAP OR DANCE?
AM I AN ASPIRING CHEF WITHOUT A CHANCE?
AM I ABANDON, DIRT, SEWAGE, AND WEEDS?
AM I AFRICA, SAND, HONEY, AND BREEZE?

AM I A FATHERLESS CHILD?
AM I ALONE IN A CROWD?
AM I A BEAST IN HEAT?
AM I AN ANT THAT SEEKS?
AM I A SOUND THAT FADES?
AM I WINE THAT AGE?
AM I A TRAIN THAT DERAILS?
AM I A REPRESENTATION OF WATER AND WELLS?
AM I NIGGER WITH A TRIGGER?
AM I A FOOL THAT SNOOZE?
AM I A BUM WITH SONGS?
AM I CHILD WITH HOWS?
AM I A PLACE OF GRACE?
AM I A TREASURE OUT OF DARKNESS?
AM I?
Shhhhhhhh
I DECIDE.

Everyone claps and seems blown away, except Malcolm, who yells out, "He stole that from Gospel Gangsters."

Leah tells him to stop hating and comes over to give me a hug. One of Ted's friends gives me twenty bucks for having the courage to recite my poem. "That's good writing."

That is the second poem I wrote before starting Grace's. My inspiration came from watching The Fresh Prince and Family Matters. The people on those shows look just like me but have totally different lives. Life is sweet for the black families on television. They have family dinner together every night, the kids get an allowance every weekend, the big brother and sister go to college, and when the kids make a mistake or struggle, the parents sit them down to correct them with love. Those television shows are like my personal church service, and they give me hope. I want that life so badly. That's why I started writing "AM I"; I know I have a gift to write poems, but I feel insecure and embarrassed that I really don't know any big words like the famous black poets.

There is a guy by the name of Jerome at my mom's church that always takes me with him to work on weekends to make extra cash. I sit in traffic with him and listen to tapes of people giving speeches without stumbling. At work, we scrub toilets and sinks in big buildings.

"When you are scrubbing toilets, think about how much you hate doing this. Then embrace it and use it as motivation for your writing. Then keep writing and I will critique it."

I am doing it for the cash, and I hate it, but for the first time I am developing a work ethic. Right there, scrubbing those toilet bowls, is where I came up with some of my poem.

....

After the talent show, I am talking to Ted when I hear screaming and banging out back. When we get outside, I realize Alvin is on the bus with Joseph's girl kissing, and Joseph is banging on the windows and doors. Joseph's friends on the team, Arthur and Antwon, are grabbing him, trying to calm him down and telling him he doesn't need any trouble with Alvin. Joseph walks away, smashing and kicking everything in sight.

"I can't believe this." You can hear the hurt in his voice.

Pooh Nigga comes running outside and yells at Alvin to come off the bus.

Ken asks what happened as Alvin steps out of the bus.

"Nothing, I was on the bus messing around with this chick."

"You know that Joseph is with her, what do you mean 'nothing'?"

Ken tells Alvin to take a walk with him, and I feel ashamed that Ted and his family had to witness this. Everyone is stirring up drama. I ask them, one by one, to chill out and just enjoy the rest of the night. I think everyone making it a big deal is scaring Ted's family.

Coach Victor is really pissed.

"We have to stop trying to kill each other; it's embarrassing. Black folks don't know how bad this looks."

I don't know how to respond to him; I feel like there is nothing I can do. For the first time on this trip, everyone is divided and goes their separate ways in the house. When Ken and Alvin come back, Alvin goes upstairs. I find Ken to talk to him.

"We have to keep Alvin on the team. He is good; we need him."

"Okay," Ken tells me, "but you have to be your brother's keeper."

"I can handle that."

When I go upstairs, Alvin, Pooh Nigga, Preston, Malcolm, Ronald, and Pookie are in the room. Some of them are plotting going over to the next room and smashing Arthur, Joseph, Elliot, and Antwon.

"You guys are crazy," I tell them. "Tell me what happened."

"I was talking to her, we start kissing, and I tell her to meet me on the bus in five minutes. So I tell Pookie to look out for me and if someone comes, just throw something at the bus. Next thing you know, Joseph is trying to get on the bus and I had to bar the door." Everyone is laughing.

"I was throwing Skittles," Pookie pleads.

"Skittles? Who is going to hear that?"

Pooh Nigga says we should wait until we get back home to start something, but I tell them to squash it because they are all scared over there. I tell the guys that we need to go down and thank the people who hosted us, so that's what we do.

We leave in the morning, and it's a quiet ride. No one says much. I sit next to Leah, and we laugh and joke the whole time. I can see that her brother is keeping his eye on us.

Every hour, Malcolm yells out to Mona Lisa. "You're not drinking right?"

"No, no honey," she tells him with her thick accent.

I like Leah, and she likes me, and I think I could just have fun with her while I wait for Grace to decide. Leah dated Arthur's best friend, so I figure she wants to do the same. After thinking about it for a few minutes, I realize I would only be wasting precious high school days. No matter what, those arrangements never end well; someone gets hurt. Above all things, Grace is the center of my heart.

Halfway through the trip home, everyone is complaining about their backs again. It's only a matter of time before Malcolm is cracking jokes on everyone. He decides to talk about the incident from last night. Everyone on the bus is laughing. Joseph jumps up and gets in Malcolm face while Mona Lisa is shouting at them to sit down. Malcolm and Joseph wrestle a bit, but Joseph can't do anything. Even though Malcolm is only a freshman, he's strong. Coach Victor yells for Mona Lisa to stop the bus, and she pulls over so fast that everyone is thrown into the back of the seat in front of them. Coach Victor tells Malcolm to get off the bus.

"But—he got in my face."

"Now," Coach Victor screams, and we sit quietly while Malcolm walks off the bus.

Joseph sits back upset and screams at his girl, "You done this." She is crying and doesn't look back. When Malcolm gets back on the bus, he sits in front with Coach Victor. After all of this typical high school drama, I have no idea what is going to happen to the team. Everything we've learned seems like it has gone out the door.

Pooh Nigga claims he has to use the bathroom bad and Mona Lisa refuses.

"Me don't stop. Pee in a bottle."

He finds an empty bottle. Pooh decides to dump the pee

out the window while Mona Lisa is driving like eighty miles-an-hour. The pee flies right back into the bus in on every-one through the windows. Everybody jumps up screaming as Mona Lisa starts swerving, rushing to the rest stop. I can't believe this trip. The rest of the way home, no one says a word.

....

When we arrive in Chicago, everyone clears the bus pretty quickly. I ask Alvin for his address and phone number.

"For sure, hit me up. Let's hang out."

"Cool. Will you be at school on Monday?"

He says he should be, and I tell him I'll see him then. I thank Coach Victor and Mona Lisa and head home. I wanted to ask Coach Victor if there will still be a team. I see the same frustration on his face that I am used to seeing from every public school teacher. My heart feels heavy with the way the trip ended. I figure I will go home and hope and pray that this team isn't over, and if it is, I will be thankful for the experience.

PART 4
LINCOLN PARK

It's the spring of 1998, and the inner city of Chicago feels energized. The Chicago Bulls made it to the playoffs and are working on their sixth NBA Championship of the decade. Last year, when the Bulls beat the Utah Jazz, the city celebrated by breaking into stores, throwing M-80 fireworks into ice cream trucks, shooting guns into the air, breaking windows, and flipping over cars. Some gang bangers even went into the Victory Outreach churchyard and set the round barrel garbage cans on fire, rolling them into the middle of the street towards traffic. The violence is getting worse every summer, and it's a miracle to be a teenager and survive until the fall.

The issue that stands out to me the most lately is that kids my age have been getting killed over their shoes. Growing up in this city, every single kid, teenager, and grown man in the neighborhood wants to be like one person. Not Martin Luther King. Not Malcolm X. Not Nelson Mandela. One man: Michael Jordan.

We can't help but think that way. When we turn on our TVs, we see Michael Jordan. When we listen to our music, the songs are about Michael Jordan. When we go to school, the first thing we hear from our teacher is a story about Michael Jordan. Michael Jordan has turned Chicago upside down with his talent.

When we watch a Bulls game, the instant the announcer says, "From North Carolina…," you can see the hair stand up on everyone's arms. If I wake up while I'm having a dream about Michael Jordan, I force myself back to sleep so the dream can continue. Those dreams feel so real. Every kid in my neighborhood says there is only one true superhero that can fly, and that is Air Jordan. I have never seen anyone in the air as long as him.

In junior high, everyone on our basketball team shaved their heads bald to be like Mike. Everyone on the outdoor basketball court dribbles with their tongues sticking out because that's what Michael does. At school basketball games, you always know the best player on the team before the game starts, because he wears number 23.

Michael Jordan is our hero. He is fearless, gifted, and gives people goose bumps—just by watching his highlights! This man takes the shots no one else will take. You can hear the city roar at every home game. Michael Jordan has already led our city to five national titles, and he gives Chicago a reason to be proud and celebrate. He is the God of our city, and people worship him.

There's a commercial that I saw when I was younger where Spike Lee asks Michael Jordan what makes him the best player in the universe. Michael Jordan is asked, "Is it the shoes"? He says no in the commercial, but I remember thinking it has to be the shoes because the entire shoe commercial is based on his ability to jump. Those shoes are the closest thing to being "like Mike."

One time, a public speaker talked to us about African-Americans in the 1960s. He told us that every time black people tuned in to their televisions, they would see Martin Luther King Jr., Robert Kennedy, or Muhammad Ali speaking. People would stop what they were doing to watch—in need of hope. "It's like they were waiting on a perfect answer," he said. So as a kid, I wanted to have a pair of Air Jordan's bad. I had the hope that I could play like him, or at least have the same image that he did. Every cool basketball player, rapper, and star on TV had a pair of Air Jordan's. Everyone in the neighborhood who had money, local fame, or women had Air Jordan's. If you had a pair, you were somebody.

Eventually, kids started saying, "Man, I would kill for a pair Air Jordan's," or, "I would die just to have a pair of Air Jordan's. I live in a neighborhood where it doesn't matter if you look like booty in the face, if you have a pair of Air Jordan's on you get a beautiful girl.

I can't afford a pair of Air Jordan's. I want to try them on so badly that I even spend a night at a friend's place to try them on while he is sleeping. Just to see what it feels like. I feel brand new, confident—"like Mike." They don't fit perfectly, and I can't suddenly jump so high that I touch the ceiling, but I still daydream that if I wear something no one else can afford that I might turn heads and girls would like me.

I know for a fact that every kid who is like me, who can't afford Jordan's, feels this way about the shoes. Now there are stories about kids getting killed over their Air Jordan's. News reports are broadcast nightly about kids walking home barefoot because someone put a gun to their head for their Jordan's. If a kid decides not to give up the shoes, they get killed. Those kids that said, "I would kill for those shoes," weren't lying. "I would die for my Air Jordan's," became the truth. I can't understand how a person can kill someone over a pair of shoes and still sleep at night. Or worse, wake up and put the shoes on their feet without being haunted. After hearing all of this, my obsession with the shoes has died, but my love for Michael Jordan is still strong. I have traded in the fantasy of being cool for some peace of mind.

The rowing team is helping me with this, but also Ken's speeches about valuing what's important in life. I want to help keep the team stay off the dangerous streets this spring, but I feel like our team is breaking after the Philly trip, even though its purpose was to make us strong and united.

....

A few days after the trip, I realize that I don't know if there is still a team. I think Malcolm might get kicked off, that a lot of people might quit, or that Ken and the coaches are going to give up on us. During our morning prayers at home, I rarely ask to pray for anything, but today I ask my mom to pray for my team: for direction, unity, and for us to learn to believe. I don't fully understand how prayers work, but I do know that when my mom prays things happen in her favor.

I leave home early and get on the Blue Line train to O'Hare, departing at the Kedzie-Homan stop. I walk a few blocks south to Lexington Ave. There are young guys already out hustling on the block; they stare me down like I don't belong. There are vacant lots and beer bottles everywhere. I arrive at West Lexington Street and a big pink building. I walk up the stairs feeling a little jittery. I ring the doorbell that says Ross Family. It's about 7:30 a.m. I ring five times until I hear a girl's voice say hello.

"Is Alvin there?" I ask.

"Who is this?"

"It's Arshay. I'm on the team with Alvin and Pooh Nigga. I, I mean Tavares." I hear a laugh, and she says I can come up. When I get upstairs, holding open the door is a cute caramel-skinned girl with beautiful white teeth.

"Hey, I'm Angie, Alvin's sister. He's in back."

I walk to the back, past the kitchen, and see Alvin lying in bed asleep with Pooh Nigga and his younger brother Robert, who he talked about a little on the trip. I'm happy to see we aren't the only family that piles up in one bed to sleep.

"Alvin, wake up."

He looks up surprised. "Boy, what the hell you doing here?"

"To wake you up for school so we can go together," I tell

him.

"Alright, give me a second."

Pooh Nigga mumbles something about how this is some "gay stuff", but I don't respond. I wait in the kitchen. On the refrigerator, I notice there is a chain wrapped around it and locked. I try to open the refrigerator to see if I can get in.

"Boy, whatchu doing?" Alvin asks. I jump back a little.

"Dude, why is the refrigerator locked down?"

He laughs and tells me that if there isn't any food, he and his brothers will actually go to school instead of staying home and starving. I nod and ask him where the rest of his family is.

"My mom doesn't live here, and my dad is at work. He leaves early to drive trucks."

On our way downstairs I tell him I met his sister, and I think she's nice.

"You get your face kicked in if you touch my sister."

"You don't have to worry about that." Alvin asks me why I came to his house, so I tell him what I told Ken.

"I will be my brother's keeper."

"Man, Ken's just lucky I'm not going to push Joseph's head back."

"That sounds painful, don't do that." We both laugh and talk about the Philly trip and the Bulls the rest of the way to school.

....

I see Grace in the hallway a few periods into the school day. I get to tell her about the spring break in Philly. She tells me that she worked all week. I admit that I missed her a lot.

"I missed you too, Molotti. Now where is my poem?"

"Not now...in time," I smile. "Are we walking to the bus stop after school?" She nods, so I tell her I will see her later. As she walks off, I look at her backside and whistle to myself. I want to ask her about Derrick but decide to wait and see if she brings it up.

I walk down to lunch and see they've moved everyone to the school auditorium. I ask security what's going on, and he tells me that the lines in the hallway to get into lunch are too crazy.

"Just go in, take a seat, and we will call you in row by row."

The girls are all sitting on one side of the auditorium and the guys on the other. I assume the lines got too crazy because the lunchroom just recently began serving nachos with melted cheese, ground beef, and jalapeño peppers, and they're super popular. Whenever the bell rings, people race downstairs to get them because they don't have enough for everybody. I also figure that the lines get so cluttered that it starts fights. I guess this is a shrewd move by security.

I'm sitting eight rows up when Alvin and some of the guys from the SOA gang stroll in. They all walk to the front and start laughing and joking around. Then Byron, one of the leaders that everyone calls White Boy because of his light skin and wavy hair, walks towards my friend Chris in the front row. White Boy grabs Chris by the shirt, snatches him off the seat, and says, "Dude, get to the back and then sit down."

Chris doesn't say a word, just puts his head down and walks to the back. Alvin and a few of the other guys push a couple more guys out of their seats and sit down, laughing. People are furious but say nothing. After a short while, they call everyone into the lunchroom. Those in back never get nachos. I sit in the lunchroom with Preston, as always, and he tells me he thinks Alvin will always be a part of them. I say, "Yeah, maybe."

After school, while I'm waiting on Grace, the football coach walks up to me.

"Hey, young fella, I would love for you to come to our summer camp and play football."

I looked at him, shocked. "Really?"

"Yeah, man. I been seeing you working out in the gym. We can use someone with your work ethic and determination."

"Determination I have to work on, but I'm on the rowing team," I tell him. He looks at me as if I'm cracking a joke.

"Listen, man, that's not a real sport, and it's not going to take you anywhere," he tells me with a finger to the chest. "Football is the heart and soul of public schools and our community. You should be a part of something big. You can row boats for fun and games."

I want to tell him that we're the first all-black row team, that's historic, and that rowing is real and harder than anything I've ever tried, but I choke.

"Okay, I will let you know," I say instead, and he slaps me on the shoulders.

"That's the spirit. I see a leader in you."

I felt a little disrespected, but I'm not going to step up to the football coach—a huge, dark, intimidating guy.

When Grace comes down, we walk to the bus stop, and I talk to her about the football Coach and how I feel. I tell her I feel like no one respects the idea of us rowing. I'm very frustrated and feel like none of the teachers respect it either. I think some parents, and a lot of the kids here, only see it as some recreational activity if it's not basketball or football.

"I respect it," Grace tells me.

"That's why you're so damn cool."

She is always supportive, always says the right things. I look at her and wonder how you couldn't fall in love with this girl. She is like the month of May in the winter time. God has blessed her with the spirit of wisdom, knowledge, and understanding. After talking to her, I sprint back to the gym as usual to get ready for row practice, hoping that the coaches are there.

When I get to the gym, I see Ken, half the team from the Philly trip, and a few new freshmen. Ken tells us the coaches won't be here today, so I ask him if they all quit. He laughs and tells me that they're just taking the day off. I take a deep breath and nod.

"Okay," Ken says, "Since the coaches aren't here, we are going to the field house for swim practice. If you have your workout gear, I'll meet you down at the bus. If you don't, take the day off."

While we're waiting by the bus, I can hear Ken on the phone yelling at Mona Lisa. He hangs up.

"I guess I'll be driving today."

"Let me guess, she is passed out somewhere," Malcolm says, and we start laughing.

The bus is still in the parking lot from the weekend, and Alvin asks Ken if he has driven a bus before or if he should call his dad.

"I haven't actually," Ken says. "Can you call him?"

Alvin calls, but his dad is still at work. Ken reassures us, "It will be fine. It's like driving a car." I feel like something is wrong with this situation, but I'm used to seeing crazier things, so I shrug it off.

We head to the field house, and it's a pretty smooth ride. People hanging out on the corners look at us like we're crazy. It is pretty unusual to see a big white school bus roll by that says "$7000" on the window and the hood. When we get to the field house, there are lifeguards there ready to teach us how to swim. It goes pretty smoothly, and we learn some new techniques. It seems like the only time the team is calm now is when we're in the water. I'm not sure if it's because the water makes us feel a sense of peace…or fear. I just know it works.

When we're done swimming, we get back on the Marshmallow Man. While driving down Roosevelt Road, Malcolm starts horsing around with the freshman in the back of the bus. Ken yells to cut it out. When one freshman gets a little rough, Malcolm grabs a bottle of baby powder left on

the bus from Philly and pours it all over him. A baby powder
cloud quickly fills up the bus, so Ken pulls into a gas station
on the corner of Independence and Roosevelt. I hear people
on the corner making jokes.

"Damn, those lil' niggas have the bus smoked out!"

"What y'all smoking?"

Ken stops the bus and yells for Malcolm and the freshmen
to cut it out before he kicks them off the team. The guys in
the back take a seat and chill out. Meanwhile, the whole gas
station is staring at the bus. People are shaking their heads,
pointing, and whispering to each other. Ken pulls out and
heads back towards the school.

Preston says, "This is ghetto."

"Yeah, you know you ghetto when you confuse baby
powder for weed smoking," Elliot tells him. Malcolm jumps
in.

"You know you ghetto when you have a hanger on your
TV as an antenna, Elliot." Everyone starts laughing.

"You know you ghetto if you still have a TV that you have
to put on U to get to the double digits," I say. Everyone starts
getting in on the joke.

"You know you ghetto when you put baby powder on your
neck."

"You know you ghetto when you stick batteries in the
freezer."

"You know you ghetto when your mom fills the bathtub
with clothes and water, and has the kids stomp on it and
pretend to be a real machine," I say.

"To come up with that one, you must really do that,"
Malcolm says, and everyone laughs. We keep playing ghetto
jokes all the way back to the school.

When we pull up to the school the block is filled with
people hanging out, girls jumping rope, boys dribbling basketballs, old men drinking beer, old ladies talking, and guys play-

ing dice. Ken makes a left into the parking lot, and we hear a crazy crunching sound as the bus lurches up and sideways. I look out the window to my left and see the bus on top of a red car. I know that this can't be good.

We see a woman and about ten dudes running towards the bus. They are screaming, yelling, and cursing, and we're all terrified. The whole block runs over. Ken seems to be keeping his cool, but I can tell he's scared. The lady is yelling up at Ken, "That's my car. Get the hell off this bus."

A guy holding up his fist says, "Come take this beating."

Ken tells us to calm down, and I say, "Let's get off and talk."

Everyone else says, "Don't open that bus door. You're crazy."

I shake my head. "I thought you guys are big time gang members that aren't scared of anything. You're gonna let this man go by himself?"

Alvin says, "Let's go."

Ken, Alvin, and I walk off the bus while everyone else stays on. The lady gets in Ken's face and says, "That's my ride."

Ken pulls out a checkbook and says, "Get a pen."

All the guys on the sidewalk watching shut their mouths as if they've never seen a checkbook before. The lady asks someone to get her a pen. Ken writes something in his checkbook and hands her the check. "No cops necessary."

She looks at the check, throws both her arms in the air as if she's about to fly, and smiles at him.

"Hey, homie, you cool with me."

"Cool."

The whole block sits and waits for Ken to move the bus, and I realize that money can get you out of almost anything.

He dislodges our bus, and it's destroyed. We ask him how much the check was written for, but he tells us not to worry about it. I am so curious to know. Alvin looks over at Malcolm, who stayed on the bus.

"What happened to you, big guy? Why weren't you out there with us?"

"I have nothing to do with that."

Ken tells us that this event stays between us, and we agree and depart the bus.

Alvin invites me over to his place to watch the Bulls game. I'm intrigued by his loyalty and know that he's the kind of friend I want. When we get to his place, we take a seat on his porch. His neighbor walks out of his apartment next door and stares us both down; Alvin acts as if nothing's happening.

"Why that dude look at us like that?" I ask him.

"It's all good. He still mad because we flipped his car over on New Year's Eve."

"What?" I ask, surprised.

"Yeah, we were bored. But we flipped it back."

"How many guys?"

"Like five," Alvin says. "He'll get over it."

I see Alvin's dad Big Al pull up, and it's suddenly like the world has changed. People who were standing in front of Big Al's house walk away. The drug addicts and dealers all wave and speak to him. All the kids pick up the trash from his yard. It's like the whole block fears him. Even Alvin changes; he seems timid.

"Hey, dad."

"Where are your sisters and brothers?"

"Upstairs."

"That's good. And the house is clean, right?"

Alvin tells him he thinks so, and Big Al says, "Well, go on and get up there."

I say hello to him and he says, "What's up." We walk upstairs into the house together, straight into the kitchen, where I say hello to Alvin's sister Angie. She says hello back without looking at me. I also meet his younger sister Diana. They all clean while I sit there, and Big Al tells jokes that aren't funny, but we laugh anyway. I think we are just laughing out of fear. Big Al takes the chain off the refrigerator and puts it in his room.

I get up and open the refrigerator to see what's inside and Alvin says, "Boy, what you doing?" and slams it closed. His sisters look at me like I'm crazy.

I sit back down and end up playing Spades with Alvin, his dad, and his brothers for the next couple of hours. The Temptations are playing on the radio the whole time; Big Al schools me on the oldies. I tell Alvin it's getting late and I want to go home and catch the Bulls game before it starts. He asks his dad if he can walk me to the train.

Big Al says, "Who in the hell is going to walk you back?" Alvin just looks shocked. His dad says he's kidding, but to come right back.

We head downstairs, and there are a few guys from Alvin's block chilling on the porch, talking about their money-making scheme. Alvin asks what they got going on and they ask him if he wants to make some money.

"Doing what?"

"Well, you know the Bulls are hot right now," this guy Tone says, "and there's a game at the United Center. What we been doing is driving the car to the game when it's over. I stand out there and see which white folks are drunk. You know they be up in the stadium getting messed up. If they pull out keys, that means they got a car. So we follow them to the car, and if they're driving, my boy will pull up with his car and drive in front of them. When they drive out into the street, he slams on the brakes.

"The guy hits us, and we jump out of car and yell at them, 'Are you drunk?' When they get scared, we tell them to give us three-hundred dollars or we calling police. Sometimes we have to go to the cash machine, but it's worth it. We make over a thousand each time."

Alvin says, "Damn."

I tell them it's really creative. "You never get caught?"

Tone looks at me, then at Alvin. "Who this?"

"He's cool."

Tone says they need another driver to make more money, and Alvin backs off. "Next time though, dog."

We both walk to the train talking about how creative they are, and about life and family. I ask Alvin why his dad talks so bad about his mom. He says it's because she doesn't support them. "But I want to kill him every time he does. Don't get me wrong, I love my dad. I just don't like when he talk about my mom."

I tell Alvin about my mom's story and about Victory Outreach, and he says that he'll mention it to his mom. I ask him how often he sees his mom.

"She comes by every other day. My mom and dad just don't speak."

We arrive at the Blue Line, and I thank him for having me over. I tell him I'll be at his place in the morning to wake him up for school.

"Dude, you don't have to do that. I'll be up."

"Cool," I tell him and get on the train.

On the way home I think about Ken driving the bus and how crazy Alvin and I are for stepping off with him. I also think about Alvin's family, and what I noticed just by being at his house for a few hours. His dad is an ex-cop with a quick temper. He has many guns hidden around the house and doesn't trust anyone. He hires drug addicts in the neighborhood to clean the yards and to fix things around the house. Big Al preaches family and says there's nothing above that. He's very old-fashioned and is the only provider in the house, so he feels like there is only one voice. What Big Al says, goes—no questions asked.

I can tell that Alvin is his favorite and that they're the closest. He says that Alvin's siblings' problems will probably land him in jail or kill him. He told me Alvin's problem is that he is too damn loyal. Alvin didn't say a word as his dad spoke. Their family bonds every day over Spades. I've never seen an immediate family so close. I think Alvin's sisters are gorgeous, and I sense that no one in the neighborhood thinks twice about crushing on them. Big Al and Alvin's brothers are fighters, and they would die to protect each other.

....

The next morning I'm at Alvin's at 7 a.m., ringing the doorbell. His sister comes to open the door, and it's the usual: chain on the refrigerator and Alvin asleep.

"Alvin, it's time to get up."

Pooh Nigga starts to stir. "Damn, dude. Don't be coming here early all in our face."

Alvin pleads, "Go to school, I will be there for second period."

"Come on, man, get up. I'll wait for you."

"I'm saying though," Pooh Nigga says, "you come here with the 'woo wat the bang,' that's not cool, but it is what it is."

Alvin says, "Yeah, I know."

I'm lost in the conversation and realize that since my mom got out of the home I haven't been hanging with the guys from the hood. I've lost my ability to interpret slang. I'm pretty sure he's trying to say that since I'm already here, Alvin should just get up and go with me.

While Alvin is getting dressed, I inspect the refrigerator to see if it will open a little bit, and it does. I'm close to grabbing a stick of butter, but it falls to the bottom. I see a couple others things down there that look like they fell, which means someone else tried to do the same thing.

On my way to lunch later, I'm walking down the hallway and get shoulder shoved by a kid named Melvin. I'm not sure if it's on purpose or accident, but I tell him to watch it. He turns around with his fist balled up and walks towards me and says, "Or what?" People around us stop what they're doing and stare at us. I look Melvin in the eyes. One part of my brain is telling me to hit him and man up while the other part of my brain is thinking about my future.

I just say, "After school."

"Cool. I will meet you after school." We both walk away.

I've never been suspended from school in my life, and I wonder what the hell just happened. If I fight this dude, I'll be suspended for sure. I think about what I told Alvin on the bus in Philly about being the bigger person, and I know I have to practice what I preach. The problem is this dude wants to fight. I just try to clear my mind and wait for the time to come. I think about trying to clear it up, but I live in a place where doing that means people will consider me a punk. I would accept that to avoid getting suspended, but I think about Grace. I know every girl in our school loves a man that can fight, but I also know that Grace isn't that kind of girl. I think about what other people will say to her or what she will hear.

When I get to the auditorium for lunch, the front two rows are empty. The third row to the back is completely full. I guess the guys are too scared to sit there because the SOA gang will embarrass them or beat them up. I decide to walk to the front and sit there. Chris and some of the guys from the crew team look at me like I lost my mind.

A minute later, some of the SOA guys come in and walk straight to the front. Everyone is looking. Alvin sits down next to me, and White Boy walks up.

"Hey, man, I saw you on the block yesterday. Al's boy, right?"

I nod yes, and he shakes my hand and sits down next to me. I swallow my spit and finally take a breath. I guess if I'm cool with Alvin, I'm cool with them.

When the last bell rings, I head downstairs to meet Grace so I can walk her to the bus stop. It's not until I see Melvin at the bottom of the stairs that I completely forgot that I had to fight someone. As I'm taking off my book bag, Melvin walks up to me and apologizes.

"Sorry about earlier. It wasn't cool; it won't happen again." He reaches out to shake my hand. I shake his hand and tell him it's all good, trying to look as though I expected an apology all along.

He walks away, and I stand there trying to figure out what just happened. I wonder if he saw me sitting in the front of the auditorium with Alvin and decided to make peace. I'm relieved because I don't want to fight Melvin. He looks like he's having a bad day just like I was when my mom told me about my grandfather. I guess every day is a bad day when you live where we live.

Grace comes down the stairs, and we leave the school together. I notice Melvin walk past Alvin and some of the guys from SOA. Alvin nods his head at Melvin and Melvin nods back, and I realize that Alvin must've heard what happened and somehow took care of it. I walk past with Grace and tell him I will see him in practice in about ten minutes. He just smiles but when I look back he's making humping gestures and laughing. I shake my head and keep walking. I don't know if I want to bring up the Melvin situation to Alvin, or leave it alone. I figure it can wait.

When I get to practice Coach Jessica has everyone sit down. She tells us she has good news. We hope she'll say we're going out of town again.

"We have a race coming up in the city," she tells us.

"In Chicago?" I ask.

"Yes, Chicago. And the Chicago Tribune will be coming to check you guys out next week."

We're blown away. She says we'll practice inside this week and get outdoor practice starting this weekend. We quickly pull out the erg machines, and everyone is pumped. While we're training, some of the guys from the football team come in and make a beat on the wall and start beatboxing "Row, Row, Row Your Boat." They start laughing and making fun of us. One of the captains, a stocky, bald dude named Colby, says, "Have fun rowing, guys."

"I can do what you do any time of the day," I tell him, "but I bet you can't last three minutes full force on this machine."

"I wouldn't waste my time. Look downstairs in the North Lawndale paper, buddy…we exist."

They walk out singing again, and Malcolm starts laughing. I tell him he has no loyalty.

"Man, chill out, they're playing."

I keep quiet and go back to training. I'm not happy at all. I take this rowing team serious. I feel like the football coach sent them in here to do that because he knows I don't want to join. After practice, I ask Alvin if he thinks the same thing and he tells me I'm overthinking it. I tell him he's probably right and head home.

When I get home, my mom seems very sad. I ask her what's wrong, and she tells me she's having problems with my little brother. "He's starting to act like his father." Then she tells me that Ike went into the home.

"They let him in? Even though he stole all those coats?"

"Yes. Forgiveness is a big part of our faith," she tells me. "I still don't know why you're so good and your brothers are so rebellious. What happened when I was away in the home?"

I tell her we pretty much did what we wanted. I want to tell her that her bad decisions have a ripple effect on us, but I know she already knows that. She's been working hard to fix that. It doesn't make sense to make her feel bad because she had a rough childhood as well.

I tell her that I learned how to be a good kid from a teacher and watching The Fresh Prince, Family Matters, and A Different World. While my brothers stayed out late, I stayed home and watched TV. I learned how to talk to my elders, what to avoid, and how to be a good friend. I was so jealous of those characters because I wanted what they had, but I loved them at the same time. I explain to her that it was like Uncle Phil became my dad, Dwayne Wayne was my brother, and Steve Urkel was my friend. They made me laugh, and I learned from their mistakes. These shows held me together during my greatest depression. I know for a fact that I am stronger because of them.

"I know that doesn't happen to everyone, but I wanted it. I just really wanted it."

She looks at me, amazed. She tells me that many are called, but few are chosen. Then she says, "I believe you are chosen," and I tell her I will talk to my brother.

Isaac tells me later that night that my mom never does anything for him, and that our grandmother is the one who takes care of him. I tell him it isn't true, and that our mom is doing her best for us now. He says he thinks that I can do whatever I want without permission.

"You hang out with friends and come in when you want; that's straight favoritism."

"Dude, every time you go out you get into a fight or cause a problem," I tell him, "If you want to do what you want, do what I do. Come home and do the dishes without being asked. Pray in the morning, stop falling asleep at church, stop getting in trouble in school, and start doing things with mom and see how things change. Until then, stop complaining."

He just says I'm lame and looks at me like I'm dumb. It seems like the more I try to become a better person for myself and others, the more haters I get. I don't care though, because I'm on a mission: to love my team more, love my family more, and love myself more.

....

All week at school, I've had nothing but rowing and preparing for the race on my mind. We've been practicing indoors and outdoors. I don't like practicing indoors because the football team and some of the other kids clown us for being on the rowing team. They tell us we're trying to be white, or come up with different boat jokes. We deal with it and try to challenge them every time.

The Chicago Tribune is coming out to see us row, and we're all pumped. When we arrive at the Lincoln Park Lagoon to row, the camera crew is already there. Coach Jessica tells us to get dressed so we can start. We stare back at her and tell her we didn't bring our workout clothes.

"Are you kidding me?" she asks.

We've all dressed up pretty nice because we know it will be in the paper. I have some nice blue jeans on, a brand new flannel shirt, and a fresh haircut. Coach Jessica looks at us, disappointed, and tells us to get to work.

The Tribune interviews Ken, Preston, and Arthur. I'm hurt because I'm not chosen to do an interview. I feel like I'm the mature and loyal one on the team, but Arthur is the team captain and Preston has a lot of personality. Preston is the coaches' favorite, and I don't stand out or have crazy talent, so I'm always on the back burner. I'm the guy who has to work really hard to get noticed, and I'm pretty sure it will always be that way for me. I'm used to it, so I just keep my feelings to myself.

I get the vibe that one guy from the Tribune is looking at us as a joke. For some reason, he keeps laughing and tapping his friend on the shoulder every time it looks like we're going to slip up. Luckily, the training goes smoothly, besides us feeling uncomfortable in our dress clothes. Afterwards, while packing everything up, Alvin comes out of the restroom upset saying he's "about to kick this white boy's butt." We ask what happened, and he says that one of the rowers from the other team said we don't deserve to be on camera. I get upset instantly. Coach Victor doesn't know what's going on, but tells us not to embarrass him in front of the cameras. I think maybe he figures we're fighting with each other. I try to open my mouth to tell him what happened, but Coach Victor says to stop or we're done. He tells us to go to the bus, so we do.

I walk into school a few days after the practice at the Lagoon, and Larry the security guard walks over and congratulates me and shakes my hand. I just look at him, confused, and ask him, "What for?" He pulls out the paper, and the whole team is rowing on the front page of the Chicago Tribune Sports section. I ask him if I can have it, and he says yes because he has a few of them. All the teachers and the principal are excited for us. Some of the guys from the rowing team are by the main office, and they are all being praised. There is a vibrant energy throughout the school, as if one of our teams just won a championship. I notice that when the teachers and staff are excited, the mood of the whole school changes. It's rare to see all the teachers so happy all at once.

Colby and a couple guys from the football team walk past, and it's a perfect opportunity for a comeback. I yell out, "Where's that North Lawndale paper of yours?"

"It's in the library, where it belongs." I can tell he doesn't know what's going on, so I hand him the Tribune with us on the front page.

"Can you put this next to it? We exist."

He looks at it, throws it back at me, and says, "Good job, niggas." We start laughing, and he goes over to shake Alvin's hand. Alvin and Colby are from the same block and have respect for each other.

When I get to class, they announce that we're in the paper.

A woman reads the article from the Chicago Tribune over the intercom so we can all hear. I pick up my paper to read along. The headlines read, "Manley's Crew Program Shatters Stereotypes about Black Athletes, But More Important, It Has a Positive Academic Impact." It is by Barry Temkin.

The woman finishes reading the article over the intercom, and everyone starts clapping. I feel like we're finally on our way. It's the first time I've been a part of something huge and I think about what Ken told us on the first day of practice: if we work hard, we will succeed. I can't wait to get home and paste the paper on my wall. The quote that sticks out to me most is "That's right, there's a crew team on the West Side, where you're supposed to dunk basketballs, not coxswains." I was so excited I couldn't stop shaking. Ken said to the Tribune that he would love to have a fast boat, but he is more interested in using rowing to keep kids in school, increase their self-esteem, and help them get admitted to colleges with good financial-aid packages. I am pumped to get back on the water.

After school, Ken and Coach Jessica are waiting for us in the back. Ken tells us that there's no more Mona Lisa and we'll be traveling to practice in his Jeep and Coach Jessica's car. They tell us who has made the final cut for the crew team: Arthur, Malcolm, Preston, Alvin, Pheodus, Pooh Nigga, Elliot, and myself. Everyone else has quit or wasn't taking the team seriously, which means we will be racing in a four boat.

We've been training hard for the last few weeks, doing laps, weightlifting, running stairs, and rowing on the erg machine until our hands are full of calluses. The erg machine is a beast, and I've been having bad dreams about it a few times a week. We start practice by rowing in a four boat and rotating between positions. We feel strong and can move the boat well, but our timing is always off so we spend a lot of time working on it. Most of the time, we are goofing off so much on the boat that Coach Jessica will stand up in the coxswain seat and let

us have it. I also notice that she is starting to feel uncomfortable with all the flirting Preston is doing with her. After practice, Coach Jessica and Ken drive us all home, dropping us off
one by one. They are both so kind, and I know they really do
believe in us.

....

Race day turns out to be a sunny morning in Chicago. We
meet at the school, with Ken and Coach Jessica arriving after
most of us. But Alvin and Pooh Nigga are nowhere to be seen
until a loud, smoking car zips into the school parking lot. We
are relieved they've made it, though Ken is curious about the
car. I tell him it belongs to Pooh, and that the neighborhood
calls it the "Illegal Pooh Nigga Regal." It's a gray Regal with
stolen plates and a muffler attached by a wire hanger.

"Is this really called the Illegal Pooh you-know-what
Regal?"

Alvin makes a face, "Man…it's Nigga."

Pooh Nigga tells Ken he can't make it because he has to
work. "But one question," Pooh shouts after Ken. "How much
was that check that you wrote that lady when the bus was on
top of her car?"

We laugh and Ken shakes his head.

We're quiet on the way to the lagoon because we're so full
of nerves. Even though practice has been going well, we're
all still uneasy because we will be the only blacks out there.
When we arrive, there are about two hundred people spread
out, and almost none of them have brown faces. We've invited our parents, teachers, staff, and some students but no one
is here, and I'm not really surprised. I had a feeling no one
would show up for us. I guess that's what Colby meant when
he said, "We exist." The football and basketball games are
always packed.

Around us, families are chilling on the grass, eating sandwiches, playing catch, and setting up seats to watch the race. There are camera crews everywhere, and I can't count the number of knots I feel in my stomach. Every rower I see looks flawless. They're tall, handsome, lean, reserved, and all wearing team Speedos. Our team decided earlier that we'd all quit before we'd wear a Speedo; Malcolm said that you can't pay a black man to wear a Speedo, and if you can, they aren't black anymore. Our uniform consists of basketball shorts, cut-off sleeve t-shirts, and headbands.

I can feel eyes burning holes through my skin, and I whisper to Preston to see if he notices too.

"Yeah, let's just have fun."

Alvin is walking around checking out the white girls, giving them winks, and trying to talk to a few of them. They just seem scared and walk off as we laugh. Ken brings us in and explains that our coach today will be Mike O'Gorman, who taught us in Philly, and that after our race there will be an erg competition. Malcolm and I will be the ones competing. Mike announces that the rowers for this race are Malcolm in four seat, Arthur in three seat, myself in two, and Pheodus in bow. Coach Jessica will be the coxswain, which means she'll help steer the boat and give us encouragement and direction during the race. Alvin and Preston aren't happy they aren't rowing, but Coach Jessica tells them they will row in St. Louis this summer. I figure it's the best decision when it comes to strength, though I'm unsure if Arthur and Pheodus are better than Preston and Alvin when it comes to technique.

"This dude is calling shots and he hasn't even been here to coach us?" Malcolm whispers to me.

I shrug, telling him to shut up. Mike tells us that there are many teams here: University of Chicago, Northwestern, different boats houses, and other high school teams. He tells us to go meet some new friends. We all think the same thing, Yeah, right. "Just kidding!" he laughs, cracking himself up.

"This dude and his Seinfeld jokes," Malcolm whispers, "not funny."

Mike explains to us that the lagoon is 1000 meters long, but we will race an 800 meter sprint race against our opponent, St. Ignatius. I look around trying to find the other team but don't see them anywhere. I can hear excitement in his voice as he tells us to take ten minutes to chill out before we come back to pre-race stretching with Coach Victor. I split off for a walk by myself while everyone else goes to check out girls. I can see that Preston and Alvin are making themselves at home talking to some girls from Kenwood High School, but they must feel pretty let down.

I stare at the city skyline on my walk, lost in thought. I look at the Lincoln Park lagoon and the Lincoln Park Zoo on the West Side. To the east of the lagoon is Lake Shore Drive, a busy expressway, and then Lake Michigan. Sometimes during rush hour, while we're rowing in the lagoon, I see people staring at us in disbelief. On my walk back I see a crowd around Malcolm and hear someone laughing. There's a journalist standing holding up a recorder while Malcolm spouts off.

"It's like Tiger Woods going into golf. It's like Venus and Serena going into tennis. It's like Jackie Robinson going into baseball or Jack Johnson going into boxing. We will dominate!"

I shake my head and walk away.

After stretching with Coach Victor, we head inside the boathouse to get our shell and start the long walk to the dock. We have never been this quiet. After we place the boat in the water, Pheodus doubles back to the boathouse. None of us know what he's doing until we see him come running back out with a life jacket on. People are giggling, and we all redden with embarrassment.

"Nigga, what you doing?" Malcolm whispers to him.

"I'm not going to drown."

None of us look up because we don't want to see the reaction from the crowd. Malcolm implores him to take the life jacket off through gritted teeth, but Coach Jessica tells us to cool down and not to make a scene.

We get into the boat and slowly push off the dock to the starting line. People stop eating their sandwiches and walk over to see us. I keep repeating to myself, It's our time. It is something they always say in church. I look out into the crowd one more time and see that out of all the teachers, friends, and parents we invited, only one person actually showed up. It's the Special Education teacher. He's a white guy, so he blends in with the crowd. I imagine that people are whispering to each other that no one came to support us.

"Ready!"

The official holds up a red flag. And it's time to race!

....

We head up to the catch, and I see the St. Ignatius team to our right, looking confident in matching maroon and white outfits, gelled hair, and perfect bone structure. One of their rowers looks back at me with a smirk, and I feel like the world is spinning. The man drops the flag and yells "Go!" and we start rowing with all our power, side by side.

Almost immediately, I can feel our boat turning to the left, the opposite way of the other team. We begin rowing harder, and I can see Coach screaming something but can't under-stand. I also see the crowd screaming. I look behind me, and— BANG—our boat slams into the brick wall of the lagoon. I can hear people saying things around me and making lots of noise. We quickly push off with our oars, and I can see that the St. Ignatius team is about three boat lengths in front of us. We quickly start rowing again, and—bang—we crash again. People are covering their mouths, trying not to scream or laugh. We stop rowing, and Pheodus starts smacking his oar against the brick. Malcolm yells out that he and I are too strong to row on the same side and he thinks someone set us up to fail. Coach Jessica yells back at him that he's being ridiculous, and everyone begins arguing with each other. I put my head down, and when I peek up the crowd is staring.

Coach Jessica says, "Okay, let's get out of this. We are going to finish this race."

Malcolm yells back, "No we're not."

"We should go back to the dock," I tell them, but when I look up and see people shaking their heads I change my mind. Now I'm angry. "Let's just finish the race."

St. Ignatius has finished the race by the time the four of us start rowing again. Behind me, Pheodus is crying. We row at straight-forward at a careful medium speed, not looking at the crowd or anywhere but the finish line. Coach Jessica is trying to calm us down by telling us we're doing well, but I can feel the negative energy seething. I'm concerned what Malcolm is going to do or say when we get off. As we glide to the end, St. Ignatius passes us going back to the dock, looking at us with no expressions. I put my head down, but Malcolm glares at them.

We continue to row without a sound and feel completely spiritless. We cross the finish line, and a few people clap for us, but it doesn't make me feel any better because I know it's out of pity. We turn and work our way back to the dock. At this point, I would pay anything to hear what my teammates are thinking. For the moment, Malcolm is completely silent. But when we pull up to the dock and Ken and Mike grab our oars to pull us in, he yells out again that we were set up to lose.

"Come on, Malcolm, keep it cool," Ken tells him in a hushed tone, but Malcolm just shakes his head no.

When we get out of the boat, Pheodus takes off running and I storm into the locker room. Malcolm and Arthur stay behind, and Preston and Alvin help take the boat inside. As I sit on the bench in the locker room, a man comes in and puts his hand on my shoulder.

"Who told you it would be easy?"

Eugene is a slightly overweight African-American man perpetually clad in an orange hoodie. He's the caretaker for the Lincoln Park boathouse, and he stands out like a sore thumb as the only black person around besides us. We never speak to him; we actually kind of make fun of him behind his back. He never says a word, but he always watches us practice, and I can tell he's proud. When I look up and see him here, I'm surprised.

"No one said it would be easy, but we clearly don't belong in this sport."

"What's your name?"

"Arshay," I tell him. He sits down next to me.

"Well, Arshay, let me tell you a story you may have heard before. There's a story of a businessman who had a ten-year-old son who consistently asked his father to take him to the park to play a game of baseball. The father was waiting on a very important conference call for work, but because of the son's persistence, the father finally agreed. He told his son to go get his glove, the ball, and the bat, and then they'd go, so the son ran up to his room with a gigantic smile and did just as his father said.

"As they approached the park, the father told his son to go out on the field with the ball and try to hit it with the bat for some practice—just for ten minutes until his conference call was over. So, the boy stood right next to home plate, with the bat in his right hand and the ball in his left. He yells, 'Pitch,' and throws the ball in the air, and as the ball is coming down he yells, 'Swing', and strike one—he misses the ball. The second time, the boy yells, 'Pitch,' and throws the ball in the air, and as the ball comes right over the plate he yells, 'Swing,' and strike two—he misses again.

"Strike three, strike four, strike five, all the way to sixteen, the boy swings and misses every time. His father has been watching every time his son misses, and he feels awful. The father ends the conference call early and walks over to his son, thinking of what he can say to comfort him. The father put his hand on top of his son's head and tells him he's sorry that he couldn't make any of those hits. The boy looked up at his father with excitement in his eyes and said, 'Dad, why are you sorry? That just means I'm a great pitcher!'"

I laugh at Eugene's story. "Told him, huh?"

"See, there is a positive side to everything, Arshay. You have to refuse to look at the negative. So what? You guys didn't win your first race, or you hit a wall. I tell you this: in ten years, no one will remember that St. Ignatius team, but people are going to remember who you guys are."

"Yeah, but that's because we ran into a brick wall."

"You seem very smart; try to get what I am saying."

I know what Eugene is saying, but I'm being stubborn.

"In no suburb, no inner city, I mean nowhere in America is it recorded that a group of black men got together in a boat to race on a crew team. You guys are the very first! Now that is history. Arshay, my friend, that is bigger than winning." He stands up. "So in this race and all the ones to come, people will remember your faces."

I tell Eugene he's a godsend, and he tells me to get back out there with my team because they need me.

"Thanks, man. We have erg races now. Will you watch?"

"With pride."

When I come out of the locker room, people are setting up the erg machines and my team is hanging out in the boathouse. Ken asks if I'm okay, and I tell him I am and I'm ready for the second part. I ask the team if anyone has seen Pheodus.

"Yeah," Preston says, "he's climbing a tree outside the boathouse."

I'm not surprised; Pheodus is a pretty weird guy and doesn't say much. When we were in Philadelphia, he barely spoke a word to anyone, so everyone gave him a hard time, including me.

"Malcolm will compete in the 1000 meters race, and Arshay will compete in the 1500 meter race," Coach Jessica tells us.

I figure Malcolm is doing the short race because he's super strong but his cardio is poor. I work very hard in practice and have the best cardio.

When we leave the boathouse, people are trying not to look at us. I know that everyone pities us, so I turn on my game face and stretch for the next round.

I feel confident on the rowing machine. It's the toughest workout I've ever done but I've learned to love it, spend time with it, and never give up while I'm doing it. Every time a friend at school thinks rowing is easy, I challenge them on the erg machine. When they're done, they have nothing but respect for the machine and sport.

What I love about it is that it works every body part at the same time. I love the sound of the fan when I'm rowing; it tells me if I'm working hard or not. Even though I literally have nightmares about this damned machine killing me, I can see my body change every day because of it. I know without a doubt that I will win this 1500 meter race because of my relationship with this machine.

The first race on the erg is between Malcolm and the guy who rowed stroke seat for St. Ignatius. We gather around Malcolm, hyping him up while the coaches prep his machine. I see Eugene, and he winks at me and nods his head. I feel a bolt of confidence ripple through me as Malcolm is strapped in. There are teams still rowing on the water, so we don't have much of a crowd. The facilitator yells up to the catch, and I look over at Malcolm. I know he will win because he is still bubbling with anger. He's got a grudge.

The facilitator is ready and gives them both the nod.

"Row!"

Malcolm's machine skips back because he pushes off so hard. Ken and Coach Victor run over and hold down Malcolm's erg because it keeps moving back with every stroke. People are amazed at how strong he is, and I can tell Malcolm is easily beating the other kid by the sound of the fan on his erg. We are all screaming and cheering Malcolm on like crazy, and for the first time I am proud of him. The look on his face says that he's here fighting for something.

He finishes, exhausted, but the other kid is still going. We are all cheering for Malcolm, and when he gets up he can barely walk or talk he is so drained. He beat his opponent by ten to twelve seconds, a lifetime in a 1000-meter race. Alvin and Arthur prop him up. The other kid from St. Ignatius stands up, and has a look on his face like, "So what, this is only a machine, why are you guys so happy? The water is the real thing."

I can't focus on him because now it's my turn. I'm racing the guy who raced on their bow seat. I am on fire with nerves, and it drives me slightly crazy that our opponents appear so calm and perfect. I sit on the machine, close my eyes, and say to myself, This is precious. I open my eyes and slide up to the catch, squeeze the handle like a vice grip, and wait for that sound.

"Row!"

I drive back with all my power and come back up to the catch at twenty-eight strokes per minute, trying to keep a good pace. I'm breathing hard and have blocked out all faces and sound. I think about making history, making movies, winning gold medals. I get hit with a wave of sluggishness and open my eyes. I can hear Alvin's voice, but I'm not sure what he's saying. I look left at my opponent's face, and I can tell he's nervous. He's all alone; it's just him and none of his teammates. Every fight I've had in my life, I have had alone; alone is home for me. I feel comfortable, and I grow so confident with every stroke that fatigue starts to leave my body. I row and row and don't look at the clock until Coach Jessica stops me.

···

"You won."

"I won?" I want to keep going.

I get up and don't make a big deal out of it; I keep my cool and shake my teammate's hands. I don't shake the other guy's hands because they didn't shake ours, but now we feel better about ourselves than we did forty minutes ago. Inside, I'm so winded that I want to collapse.

Coach Jessica lets us know there are snacks in her car, and we all run over. Pheodus is still on top of his tree. I yell for him to come down, and he tells me he'll come down when he's ready. Alvin says, "Man, if you put that fool's brain in a bird it would fly backwards."

When we get to the car, there are apples and fruit bars. I had never eaten anything healthy until I started rowing, and it feels great. The healthy food makes me feel light on my feet. My mind is always clear now, and I swear I'm less lazy.

"You missed it, Arshay," Alvin tells me. "Malcolm was going to beat up one of the guys."

"Really? What happened?"

Malcolm says, "One of the guys came up to me saying its tradition when we lose to give up our shirts. I stepped up to him and said 'come take it,' and he just kind of ran off. I don't care if it is tradition; someone made us lose."

"Man, Mike is one of the best coaches in the sport," Preston pipes in. "You guys lost that race."

"So I guess our rowing team is more like Michael Jordan going into baseball," I say to Malcolm, and everyone starts laughing.

"More like Charles Barkley going into golf."

"More like Shaq going into movies."

Malcolm laughs. "I deserve that one, but Coach Jessica should have picked our positions." We agree. I know that Mike is the best coach that has taught us, but he just isn't around to see how we're doing. I knew he's legit because he's Coach Jessica's rowing coach. I know that's why she trusted him with us.

We hang by the zoo until Ken and Coach Jessica are finished checking out the other races. She takes Arthur and Pheodus home, and Ken takes Alvin, Preston, Malcolm, and me out to dinner somewhere in the West Loop. When we get out of Ken's Jeep, there are a lot of really nice restaurants around. I know these places are considered fine dining, which I've been learning about in school. The host at the first restaurant tells Ken we can't come in because we aren't dressed for the evening. Ken looks incredulous.

"There are people in there wearing t-shirts and jeans, just like my guys."

"Well, they're not twenty-one."

"Oh? Now it's their age?"

I had a feeling this was going to happen, so we pull Ken away, but he is visibly upset. Malcolm calls the host a "racist bastard" and we walk off. Ken is not like any other white guy I've ever met. He does what he wants and has a little ghetto in him; he never backs down from anything. We walk down the street until we find a nice place that lets us in. There is something disturbing about thinking that they're being so accommodating just by letting us in. We're good kids, and that seems so backward.

Ken takes us to One Sixtyblue, which is owned by Michael Jordan. The service staff is dressed in crisp black and whites, and they greet us warmly. The host brings us to a beautiful table covered with a white tablecloth with a large candle in the middle. The waiter comes by to introduce himself and gives us each a really big menu. I don't understand a single selection on the menu.

"You in cooking class and you don't understand this?" Preston asks.

"I don't yet, but I will one day. I know the names of six different wines and their colors."

Ken is impressed with that and gives me a high-five.

While I'm looking at my menu, it catches on fire because I have it resting on top of the candle. Ken puts it out, and I am mortified. The guys are laughing at our first fine dining experience and how wrong it's gone already. When the waiter comes back with our water in a wine glass we all start goofing off. We put on "proper" voices, swirl the wine glass, and talk about our experiences in Harvard and Yale. When we realize the prices on the menu we ask Ken if we can have the money instead and just go to Burger King. He laughs and tells us no because life is about experiencing new things.

When the waiter takes our orders, Preston asks for the filet mignon but pronounces it totally wrong. Alvin asks for the New York strip steak, and then asks to substitute the sides for another New York strip steak. The waiter starts laughing, but we don't because we know he is serious. Malcolm and I both play it safe with pasta. It was always a dream of mine to eat at a fancy restaurant. Now that the dream is fulfilled, there is room for more dreams.

Now I want to work at one.

It's a beautiful dinner. Ken talks to us about what happened at the race today and says that he wants the four of us to start taking his youth entrepreneurship classes. I feel really close to the guys and know that the moment we experienced pain together, we became a team. We feel the same agony because we care about the same thing.

I am grateful to Ken for making all this happen and starting a program that will call for criticism. I faced a fear of water, and now life is a little less scary. He is a special kind of human being. We respond differently with him than we do with anyone else. We are so used to people we encounter talking at us. Nagging us, yelling at us without knowing anything about us. They tell us to do things but don't want to take the time to get to know us. Ken always talks with us. He spends time with us, learns our jokes, our ways, our inner strengths and weaknesses. Ken uses his time, talent, and treasure to get to know us.

It's like a bank account: You have nothing to withdraw if you don't make a deposit. A lot of times teachers and parents just want to withdraw from us. They want to know our problems, secrets, and the things that are going on in our lives. They wonder why we never tell them anything, and the reason is because they've never made any deposits. Ken is excellent at making trust and faith deposits in our lives.

PART 5
ST. LOUIS

When I was fourteen years old, Vince Alanis from Victory Outreach told a story about a chicken and an eagle.

There was a majestic golden-eyed eagle that had just laid an egg in her nest. Soon after, she flew away to find food. A strong wind came and blew the nest down, and the eagle egg rolled over into a chicken coop. The egg hatched, and the eagle grew up around the other chickens in the coop. He spent his whole life thinking he was a chicken, he clucked like a chicken, walked like a chicken, and he was raised by the other chickens. One day, a giant eagle flew into the chicken coop and asked the young eagle, "What are you doing with these chickens?"

"What are you talking about? I'm a chicken."

The other eagle said, "Look into my eye."

In the reflection, the eagle saw that he looked just like the other eagle and not like the chickens.

The two eagles left the coop together, and the chicken eagle was shown everything he was born to do. He saw that the older eagle had to ability to fly higher and faster than he had ever done. He saw that the eagle could see far into the distance, and was so strong that he can lift a full grown fox. It was clear to him that he was born with greatness he'd never known, and that he could live a life with no limits. That same greatness had existed inside of him, but he was limited by his surroundings and those around him. Living around those chickens, he had never tapped into his own greatness.

I could relate to this story because I considered myself a chicken for a very long time. I did the same things every day, got the same bad grades, and hung out with the same knuckleheads day in and day out. The highest goal I set for myself was to cook in someone else's restaurant. I was trying my best to be different, and I truly believed that going to jail and being broke wasn't normal. I also refused to believe that becoming a rapper or a basketball player was the only way to make a living. I knew somewhere deep down that I was born for greatness, but because of my surroundings, I couldn't see it. I didn't know I was good at writing poems, having self-control, thinking big, being creative, or having a strong work ethic until I got away from my friends who only wanted to chase girls.

I had lived my life as a chicken, but I knew I could be an eagle.

The school year is coming to an end, and all year Ken and Coach Victor have been like that majestic eagle who flew into the chicken coop to remind us we were born for greatness. Ken introduces us to successful black men and women to share their stories. He pushes us to our limit and beyond. He no longer has us practice at the school; we only row at the Lincoln Park lagoon, far outside of our neighborhood. Ken plans for all the future crew races to be outside of Illinois. When Ken takes us out for dinner, he picks neighborhoods in the city that are very different from our own.

Ken sets up summer jobs for me, Preston, Malcolm, and Alvin at the SAFE Foundation in Chicago. He tells us that we will all have a job giving back to kids and being a leader. Ken's idea for us is to mature over the summer by working with inner-city kids and becoming their mentors. I can't wait for the school year to finish so I can start.

Ken believes in us, but I know that we need to start believing in ourselves too. I try to challenge my teammates to be better in everything we do. I see the car Ken has, the way he inspires people, the programs he's started, the pictures of his beautiful wife, the huge company he owns, and I want a life like that. I looked at my mom life and wanted the worked ethic and peace that she has.

··

I am heading to meet Ken at his home in the West Loop to work out on a Saturday morning, and when I turn onto the 1500 block of Ashland I'm completely blown away. The block looks just like the one from The Cosby Show. The buildings are enormous. I'm amazed but also not surprised that he lives on this gorgeous block.

I ring the doorbell, and his wife comes to the door. "Hi, I'm Jeni. Come on in." Jeni is pretty and looks a lot like Jennifer Love Hewitt with the same long dark hair. Looking at her, I can't believe it's the same person who is always calling Ken screaming. One time, Ken was dropping us all off at home after practice. We were at a stop light in the middle of a gang-infested West Side neighborhood on Independence and Polk Street when Ken's phone rang. We could all hear Jeni screaming on the other end. Ken hung up and looked at us.

"Guys, hop out of the car. I have to get home to my wife."

We looked at him like he was joking.

"Not here, man," Malcolm said. "Did someone die?"

"No, you don't know my wife," Ken said, shaking his head. "Here is twenty bucks, I have to go." We got out of the car and shook our heads.

"Damn! That woman must be crazy."

Their eighteen-month-old daughter Winnifred is crawling around. I'm the first one here, so I play with her for a bit and try to teach her my name. I am in love with their home, a four-story brownstone with chandeliers, a library, and a gym upstairs. Jeni is chilling in the dining room with a book, and once Malcolm, Preston, and Alvin arrives she heads upstairs. I want to thank her for lending her husband to us; in church they always say "behind every good man is a great wife." But I get too nervous to say anything. She seems so tough.

I tell the guys that I don't think she likes us.

"Of course not," Malcolm says, "she's a—,"

"—racist," we all say and crack up. He thinks everyone is a racist, so it's not hard to finish his sentences. Malcolm picks up Winnifred.

"And this little one thinks we're aliens!"

Ken tells us it's time to go. When we ask where, he tells us the East Bank Club.

"It's the biggest gym in Chicago. Oprah Winfrey and other celebrities work out there."

"Oprah?"

I tell Preston we have to find Oprah and tell her we're the first black rowing team so we can be on her show. He says okay in a sarcastic voice, and everyone starts cracking up.

"Whatever, you guys are dream killers."

When we get to the East Bank Club, it feels like I'm walking into a mall. There are stores, big restaurants, people everywhere. Ken shows us around the place, upstairs to the huge indoor running track that wraps around the building, and down to the mammoth basketball courts. The main floors have big screen TVs everywhere, and the men's locker room feels as though I am in an ornate hotel lobby; it is overwhelming.

"Okay, guys," Ken says, "I am going for a run, and I want you guys to work on the erg machine and run track."

We nod in agreement, but as soon as he leaves the locker room we run straight to basketball court.

There are some actual Harlem Globetrotter players practicing on the court, so we sit and watch them for a few minutes before we start playing. I notice that Alvin isn't much of a basketball player. After a couple games, I try to get some of the guys to go look for famous people with me but they just want to go to locker room to watch TV. When we walk into the locker room lounge area, there are naked old white men everywhere. We've never seen anything like it and are basically vomiting in our shirts.

"Look at that dudes butt." Preston blurts out. "That's nasty."

I am so embarrassed I want to hide in one of the lockers. Hanging out with the older guys from church makes me a little more mature, so I don't goof off as much—but I still can't stop from laughing.

When we sit down, there are three middle-aged white men in towels watching baseball and chatting. Their conversation is way over our heads. They are talking about hedge funds, investments, country houses, and yachts so Malcolm, Preston, and Alvin start mocking them in their best white guy voices.

"Hey, Todd Myers, I sent my daughter to Harvard and for crying out loud she dropped out and became an artist."

"Well, Bob Chuckles, for the love of God, she needs a good backhand."

"Fellows, it's really not that bad. I myself lost six million yesterday, and my wife left me and took the yacht."

The white guys are turning red in the face trying not to say anything, and I can't stop laughing. The guys get up suddenly and mumble something I can't understand, but they are clearly pissed off. Malcolm takes the remote and changes the channel to BET, and we sit there to watch. I wish I had the strength to tell the guys to cut it out, but I don't. We are growing as a team, but we're still immature in a lot of ways. I know we have to learn how to act in certain places. I can't get the image out of my head on how cool, calm, and collected the rowers from the other teams were. From what I've seen, crew teams are all first class, elite people. They believe in themselves, their backgrounds, and their teammates. I am longing for the day that we become as disciplined as those other teams.

··

After we leave the East Bank Club, Ken begins to educate us on the sport of rowing and its rivalries. He tells us about rowing in Boston at the Head of the Charles River. The Head of the Charles Regatta is the largest two-day rowing event in the world. Ken tells us about the energy of the event; people yell and throw things, and there is a fervor that few in the world will ever experience. He talks about the feeling of a 2000 meter boat race, which is typically five and a half to seven and a half minutes.

"It's a non-stop sprint," he says, "moving in sync with seven other guys in the same motion for seven minutes with no breaks whatsoever."

I tell Ken that I've gone a day without eating, been in fist fights, been beaten with belts and cords, been tackled on a football field, and been hit upside the head with a glass bottle, and none of it hurts more than a 2000 meter race on an erg machine when you're giving your all. I ask Ken why rowing is never on sports channels, or in local papers.

"I guess people don't consider it exciting," Ken shrugs.

"Well," I said, "once everyone sees the Head of Charles Regatta, maybe they will change their minds. I'm sure ladies love seeing men in tights, and men love seeing women in tights. People love being by the water, it's a great family event, there's no blood, and to see the waves and splashing of water is beautiful."

I can tell the other guys are getting annoyed with my questions, but Alvin says, "I love how the coxswain is screaming and yelling to motivate the guys on the boat. I will be cursing everyone out."

Preston asks Ken what a regatta is, and he says it's a side by side race.

"You know, like we did at the Lincoln Park Lagoon. There are also head races which take place in the fall. Boats begin with a rolling start at intervals of ten to twenty seconds and are timed over distance. The regatta is more of a sprint, and head races are more of a marathon." Hearing about racing in Boston is fascinating to me; it's like hearing about the Holy Land. Most people will only dream about it. It becomes a goal for me, and I'm hoping my ambition will be contagious to my teammates.

Ken drives us to the West Side to drop us off, and we arrive at Alvin's place first. When we get to the stoplight, a few of Alvin's boys are standing on the corner and see Alvin in the car. When they see Ken driving, they look back at Alvin.

One guy says, "Dude, you not riding with The People, right?"

Alvin shakes his head no, but they still seem confused. I ask Alvin why they call the cops The People but Ken answers.

"Arshay, if you go to court today, the case will be called The People vs. Arshay Cooper. It's you against the system."

We pull up to Alvin's house and drop him off. Alvin's dad is happy that he's part of something but also suspicious. His dad is very old school and asked me and Alvin last week why we hang out with Ken so much. He asked if Ken is touching us, and we both tell him, "Hell no." Alvin's dad says he doesn't trust Ken because no white man just helps people without expecting anything in return. I want to defend Ken, but Alvin's dad is so scary I don't want to speak up and tell him he's wrong. I can see Alvin is slowly changing, but it's hard with his dad having that old school "we're all we've got" mentality. Alvin told me once that crew is the best time he's had in sixteen years of living.

We drop Malcolm off next. Malcolm has five brothers and three sisters, and only two have moved out. They are all street smart and love to debate. Malcolm's dad is Muslim and has passed on most of his theories to Malcolm, and his mother is elderly and very sweet. I once told Malcolm that I don't know why he came out so bad. Every time his mother sees me she always says, "Come here, boy, you got so fat." There are times she just hears me coming in and says it before she even sees me. I think I'm as lean as chicken breast!

Malcolm's family is excited that he's on the rowing team and not at home stirring up trouble, but we have to deal with him stirring up trouble on the team. There are times I wish Malcolm wasn't on the team because of his mouth, but he is too damn strong to not be an asset.

Next, we drop off Preston, still everyone's favorite. He's the kind of guy that gets everything right the first time. He loves the rowing team and flirts with Coach Jessica nonstop. Coach Jessica removed Preston from stroke seat because when she steers the boat he can't keep his eyes from her legs. He is a sex addict, along with Alvin, and both of them are tied for hooking up with the most girls during freshmen year.

The guys on the team clown Preston mom because she always looks like she's smoked a couple blunts. I've noticed lately that Preston is slipping in school and smoking weed all the time, and he's started saying that he is a Conservative Vice Lord. That's one of the local neighborhood gangs. I took Preston to church with me a couple times, hoping that he could learn some of the positive things I've learned, but to no avail. Preston refuses to do what I do: to let go of the "friends" from the neighborhood.

Lastly, Ken drops me off. He's met everyone else's family many more times than mine. The team jokes that I don't really have a home because I never let them in, but my apartment is so small. They say I'm becoming less hood every day. Malcolm always calls my mom Sister Betty Shabazz because all she does is work and church, and I'm okay with that. She learned to provide for her kids, and church provides for her spiritually and mentally. My step dad Ike went into the home but left a week later and started back on drugs. My mom has come to terms with being a strong single parent.

I really believe that people didn't understand how much I learned from watching Family Matters, The Fresh Prince, and A Different World. Dwayne Wayne's character taught me that no matter how hard school gets or no matter what people say about your physical appearance, push through it and be yourself and always give back to place that gave to you. Steve Urkel's character taught me how to love a girl and the importance of patience. The Fresh Prince taught me how to be a good son, and to be afraid to do wrong because no one gets away with anything. I practice everything I learn from these shows in my daily life, and I get positive results.

I also see what is missing in my life: a trusted teacher, a father figure, a mentor, friends that are positive and loyal. I decided to seek those missing pieces because they aren't necessarily around me. I joined a team of brothers, I go to church on my own time to hang with positive influences, and that night while Ken drops me off, I ask if I can go to his place tomorrow to hang and learn more about rowing. He tells me I can if I will help him clean out his garage. I jump out of Ken's car, ecstatic over the brotherhood that he has built.

Never in a million years would we be hanging out together otherwise, but crew unites us with Ken and we practice almost every day. Eugene, the caretaker from the boathouse, calls us the Black Oarsmen Crew and I'm starting to consider myself the captain.

....

The next morning when I get to Ken's place, he's upset that someone stole his bike from his garage.

"From here? This is a nice neighborhood."

"Yeah, this is where they go to steal. No one is going into

the inner city to steal someone's bike."

We decide to go for a run, and Ken has me chill with Winnifred while he goes to find workout clothes for me. I play with Winnifred for a few minutes, and I'm shocked when she remembers my name; she is a very smart baby. She is so cute and only crawls with one hand. I pick her up and toss her in the air. She starts crying, and I realize she isn't the type of kid that likes physical play. She's a little fancy.

When Ken comes down he says, "Did you pinch my daughter?"

"No, man, I didn't!"

"Arshay, I'm kidding," he says, laughing at me.

I let out a sign of relief.

"Come on, man, you can't play like that."

Ken yells upstairs to Jeni that he's leaving, and she yells back that he should bring Winnifred upstairs.

"Hey, Jeni," I yell up to her.

She says hello back in a strange tone. I can't help but think that this woman does NOT like me.

I change clothes, and Ken and I head out on our run. We pass Malcolm X College, United Center, Crane High School, and head towards the Rockwell Gardens Projects. There are a few guys standing outside; I'm not sure if they are selling drugs or just hanging out. It is early, so I assume they are selling drugs.

As we run past them, one says, "Look at this cracker."

I know that we're in the projects, so the best plan is to just keep it moving, but Ken stops running. I see him walk back to the guy and stand face to face.

"Who you talking to?"

There's a few of them, and I am not happy that Ken decided to stop.

The guy steps down though. "My bad, man, it's all good."

Ken gives him a nod and starts running again. I want to

tell him how stupid that was, but I keep my mouth shut. Ken is completely fearless, and I keep wondering where he gets his confidence or his pent-up craziness.

....

One time, about a week after our first race, Ken took us to the University of Illinois at Chicago to go bowling and all the pins got stuck. So he walked down the bowling lane to line up the pins himself while we are yelling that he can't do that. The staff is even yelling that he can't do that, but Ken does what he wants when he wants. With Ken and the team hanging out a lot, we notice things that white people can do that blacks can't get away with, and things black people can say that white people can't. It's a trip.

When we get back to Ken's place after the run, we start working on the garage. He tells me everything he knows about rowing and his entire experience racing in college. He tells me how he wants to retire from trading sooner rather than later and spend his life teaching and building Urban Options. He tells me a career is awesome, but there is no greater calling than helping kids and giving back. I ask a lot of questions about starting a business and he tells me what he knows and even prints out some stuff he thinks will help me. I tell him how I want to be a chef, and he tells me he has a friend that is a cook.

"Not a cook. A cook is employed in a chef's kitchen. I want to be a chef, but not a regular one, a traveling chef or something."

"Let me know what you need to get there," Ken says. "Just keep taking my entrepreneurship classes. How are your grades?"

"They're okay," I shrug. "I just have an issue staying focused. All I think about is rowing or Grace."

"Those are not bad thoughts, but sometimes it is good to

have tunnel vision."

"What's tunnel vision?"

"Tunnel vision is focus," he explains, "limiting what you see or think. When you're in a tunnel, you can only go one way. When you're in school, think about school. When you're with Grace, think about Grace. When you're rowing, think about rowing."

"Wow. That helps, because my mind is always all over the place."

Ken tells me he taught a class at Manley and met Grace. "She is a sweetie pie."

"I know, but I don't think I have a shot."

"Patience is a virtue, Arshay."

I ask Ken about Jeni and tell him I don't think she likes us very much. "Does she think we're freeloaders or something?"

"No, not at all. Jeni is a firecracker who takes nada from no one, and she's also busy with law school."

"How is she a firecracker?"

Ken laughs aloud. "Where do I start?"

He tells me about a time that they went to the movies in North Lawndale. While they are in the theater, Jeni got up to use the restroom. He says about ten minutes passed, and he heard some screaming and yelling outside the theater and knew it was her. Ken says that when he stepped out, there was security everywhere and Jeni was charging three women. One of the girls had been beating her kid in the bathroom and Jeni told her to stop.

"Damn! She is a G."

"I love her," he shrugs. "She is a unique individual that never backs down. We're both fearless, and we understand the world the same way. She's going to be a criminal defense attorney, and she will be the best at it."

I stay over late and have dinner with Ken, Jeni, and Winnifred. We bond and Jeni explains to me what Criminal

Defense is, and about the job she'll be doing. I tell Jeni about Grace and how I think that even if I get to be with her I know I won't know what to do.

"What do you mean?" she asks.

"Grace is smarter, very good-looking, and she's been dating. I just don't know how to entertain her or be a cool boyfriend."

"You're insecure. There is no reason to be insecure." Ken tells her to relax, but she keeps going. "No, don't tell me to relax. Arshay, there is no reason to be insecure. You go get what you want."

Just like that, she gets up from the table and heads towards the stairs.

"I have to get some work done."

Ken looks across the table at me.

"Welcome to my world."

....

On the drive home, I tell Ken something that no one but my mom knows.

"When I was in eighth grade, I didn't pass the state test to make it to high school. I was supposed to make a 6.8 reading and math level to pass." I take a deep breath.

"Things were so messed up at home that I couldn't even read a paragraph without thinking about how bad life is. I was so focused on how to be cool for the kids at school that I couldn't focus on adding numbers. I would have a painful night and then go to school the next morning and have to read some bland fiction.

"I messed up that test on purpose by turning it in when everyone else did to not seem dumb. I didn't even try. So I failed, but they let me walk across the stage. They told me I had to go to summer school for the bridge program and I can go to high school if I pass there, but I also failed the test in summer school. Not because I purposely failed, but because I felt like I wasn't smart enough. I tried, but my mind is always elsewhere. So I was told I had to repeat the eighth grade and if I did well by Christmas break they would place me in high school."

This all happened right around the time my mom graduated from the recovery home. I was so embarrassed that all the friends that I hung out with, laughed with, and fought alongside would be going to high school without me. I felt even dumber. So I told my mother to transfer me to an elementary school far away so we could move out of the neighborhood. I purposely lost contact with every single friend at William Penn just so I could focus. I didn't really forgive them for making my life hell anyway. So with no friends around I was able to focus and learn. Hanging with some church guys every once in a while helped too. I read my first book, The Count of Monte Cristo. That was a big accomplishment for me.

"After that, I passed with flying colors and went back to my correct grade. I believe it's a combination of my mom getting her act together and me making a choice to trade in fun for my future."

Ken is amazed. He tells me he is proud of me and says I will be a good team captain one day. I get out of the car but turn back.

"Just one more thing,"

"What's that?"

"How much was the check you gave that lady for the bus cr—,"

"Get out of here!"

I'm cracking up as I head inside, happier and more confident than I've ever been. Ken is undoing what all the bad teachers and friends did to my self-esteem. Watching his actions and seeing the man he is to his family gives me hope.

....

I've been to Ken and Jeni's place every weekend for the past month to hang out and pick Ken's brain. Jeni and I have gotten pretty cool, and we bond a lot over rap music. Every rap CD I want, she has. Jeni is passionate about Tupac, getting innocent people out of prison, and being a realist. It is bizarre to me that Jeni and I are from two totally different places and generations, yet share the same exact sense of humor.

One weekend, Jeni takes me to Bloomingdale's to shop with her and Winnifred. When people see us together, they give us a funny look and then peek at the stroller to see what color the baby was. I guess there aren't many thirty-year-old white women walking around with sixteen-year-old black men in Chicago and pushing strollers. I even get dirty looks from black girls. On our way down to the parking garage, one lady walks up to look in the stroller and is being very obvious.

"Strong genes," I say. Jeni bursts out laughing, and the woman's face goes crimson.

Spending time with Jeni has shown me that I really like her, and I think she is exactly what Ken needs. She's strong, organized, uncompromising, fearless, powerful, and intelligent. I can also tell that when you truly get to know her and win her heart, you reap the benefit of her sweetness and protection. She is the type of person you love not because of what she's done, but because of who she is. While my mom works and my siblings hang out with their friends, I enjoy hanging with Ken and Jeni. They say the house feels more alive when I'm around.

It's the last few weeks of school and also race week. The plan is for me, Preston, Malcolm, and Alvin to race while Coach Jessica coxswains. We still haven't found a person small and responsible enough to steer the boat. I love when Coach Jessica steers the boat because she is great at motivating us, and I'm a little nervous because Preston and Malcolm missed a few practices in the last week. I start getting stressed because I'm thinking about our last race and that brick wall. I decide to take the leadership role and stay on top of Preston and Malcolm about taking this race serious. Malcolm starts calling me "Ken's pet" because I stay on his case so much.

The night before we leave for our second race in St. Louis I ask Alvin to drive me by Grace's place to hang out. Alvin is the only one that has a driver's license on the team, and he drives the Illegal Pooh Nigga Regal. Alvin is slowly changing but still has his thuggish ways. One thing I like is that he is always supportive and always willing to go out of his way.

When we pull up to Grace's block, Alvin gets a crazy look in his eyes, and I know it's because there are gangstas and drug dealers everywhere.

"Dude, you take the bus over here for this chick?"

"Yeah man, I know. It's pretty scary."

Alvin comes in with me to Grace's apartment. Her mother, Karen, is incredibly gracious. While I'm talking to her, Alvin is trying to get my attention by making hand gestures and urging me to take Grace to her bedroom to make a move. I try not to laugh. He is all about hitting and quitting, but that's not my style. I take Grace to her room to talk, but before I can say anything she speaks first.

"I know it's been months and you've been patient. You are the sweetest person I know." She kisses me on the cheek.

"Yeah, no problem," I say, feeling like a sucker.

"When I'm ready, it will be good."

I want to tell her that I feel like we're spinning in circles, and it's time to make something happen. Instead, I tell her that once she decides if it's going to be a yes or a no, only then will she get the poem I wrote.

When Alvin and I leave, he asks me if I ever plan on trying to have sex with Grace. I tell him that I do, but it's a process. I must sound frustrated because he tells me he always has somebody else for me.

"I don't like somebody. I like Grace."

Sex is one thing I don't like talking about. It's too confusing. I go to church and everyone says stay away from it, it's not godly before marriage, you can suffer from a disease, broken heart, or delaying your future by having a child. I see all these things happening. But when you turn on the TV, music videos show you how good it feels, the radio makes you want to have it all the time, and the guys at school will clown you if you don't. I'm not having sex, so when it comes up I just turn away.

Alvin heads to the Burger King drive-thru for a burger. I tell him we can't be eating this food anymore.

"Dude, it's just a burger."

Alvin is so smooth that he gets the cashier's phone number at the first drive-thru window, and then drives down a couple feet to the second window and gets that girl's phone number too—with the same exact lines. I can't help but laugh.

On the way home he drops a bomb out of nowhere.

"You know what? I was going to kill my dad last night."

"What! Why?"

"I can't tell you right now, but I have a knife in the bathroom. I was crying and waiting for him to go to sleep."

I can see him start to tear up.

"My little sister said she was down to do it with me. But I don't want her involved, so I'm going to wait."

"Alvin, if it's something major, you have to say something."

"No man, it's all good."

I think maybe his dad beat him or said something about his mom. I ask him if he told his mom about Victory Outreach yet. He says he hasn't, but he will.

Alvin drops me off, and I tell him I will be at his place early tomorrow as usual. He thanks me. When he pulls away, I sit on the porch to think about all the things I used to go through at home, and how nobody knew. I think about how I wasn't really alone, that it's possibly happening to every young man and woman I know in my school and in my city. My mind is filled with voices that I've heard in the last year from the guys at church, the guys at the barbershop, my mom, and Ken. Those voices are talking about change and the responsibility of reaching out to those who are hurting. I want to be an agent of change for my teammates and those around me but I feel a little bit like I have one foot in and one foot out because I'm still young and want to be cool. But in the hood, the cemetery is full of young guys who wanted to be cool.

The next morning after our daily family devotion, I pick up Alvin. He seems to be doing better. We head to school, and I can't wait until it's over and we drive to St. Louis. When the final bell rings, we run outside and jump in Coach Jessica's car. Coach Jessica's friend Mandy from her rowing team is there as well, so Alvin, Malcolm, and I ride with Mandy, and Preston rides with Coach Jessica. We say Preston is "living the dream" and start laughing.

It's a long six-hour drive. On the road, we see other rowers with stickers on their cars and some trucks with boats on top. We're reminded that this is a big event. Mandy talks a lot about books, and I tell her I read a few books a month because there is a guy at my mom's church that gives the teens twenty dollars every time they read a book that he lends them.

When we get to St. Louis, we get dinner and then check into our hotels to rest. Once we're unpacked, the guys start getting the pre-race jitters. I remind them that if we win this race we will make the papers again. They all agree with me and say they feel ready.

We're all in shock the next morning to see how beautiful the Creve Coeur Lake is. It's much bigger than the race we had in Chicago. It is amazing to me that all rowers seem the same: tall and lean with beautiful face structures. Everyone is representing their team colors on their spandex. We are all dressed the same with basketball shorts, t-shirts with cut-off sleeves, and headbands. There are a lot of people stretching and hanging out until their race time, so we walk around checking out the female rowers. Everyone is looking at us, and we are turning a lot of heads. We walk past a guy interviewing a team with a tape recorder.

Alvin yells out, "Don't want to interview the Black Oarsmen?" Preston tells Alvin to chill.

"Guy's, let's just race and get out of here," I tell them.

Malcolm shrugs. "I'm here for the experience. We're not about to win any races."

"Kill the stinking thinking," I say.

....

Malcolm and Preston split off. Alvin sings to every girl he sees, and they smile and keep walking. I walk over to the dock to check out some of the cool boats I saw on the way down. I wish that I knew more about this world; everything is so foreign, and water is something we've always been told to stay away from. My experience with water is that it's never cold enough when you drink it, and never hot enough when you're washing clothes, or hands, or dishes. My biggest water memory was going to the local pool where the older guys forced us under water until we couldn't breathe. All in all, I'm not too fond of water. I reread the Chicago Tribune article about us almost every day, and what sticks out the most is when the writer says we are "dipping our toes into very foreign waters." Every time I practice, and before I get into the boat, I say to myself, "Okay, this is foreign water."

While admiring the boats, I hear someone approaching me, a stringy white guy with bright orange curls. He was the one interviewing the other team. He asks if I have a second, and I say sure, but my coach is just outside the boathouse.

"It's okay, just a few questions." He puts the tape recorder near my face. I can see Alvin walking over.

"So they say the Black Oarsmen will change the sport."

I just stare at him because I'm not sure if he's serious or sarcastic.

"No, we're just changing our lives."

"Is this your first race? And are you nervous?"

"No…and no."

"What makes your team different from everyone else?"

I blink at him while holding in a loud laugh, and then slowly look around at every other rowing team there. I say into the recorder, "We wear headbands."

Alvin is cracking up, and the reporter just nods his head.

"Does your team have any goals?"

"Hopefully we win and make history."

He thanks me and walks off.

Alvin shouts after him, "What about my interview?"

"Next time," the reporter yells back.

Alvin tells me that all my time with Ken has made me quick with my speech.

"Nah, man, I've just been dealing with people talking trash all my life."

As we walk away, it occurs to me what we've been missing. I think the problem is that we haven't set any goals as a team; we're just going day by day. My mother always says people perish without vision. I think that applies to our team too. I'm a true believer that if you have a bow and arrow and aim for nothing, you will hit nothing every time. We need a clear target, a clear goal. Ken talked to me about vision before, and having the ability to focus on what you want and then get it.

....

Closer to race time, the weather changes. It is cloudy and a little wind picks up. There are even waves on the lake, but it doesn't look too scary after watching the previous races.

Coach Jessica tells us to take a knee on the grass.

"Guys, we've had some good practices. Remember it's about drive and recovery on the boat: drive back with power and recover on the way up. When you recover correctly, you will have a powerful drive. There are some waves out there, so I want you to concentrate on full, powerful strokes and timing. I don't want you guys catching a crab out there."

I'm terrified of catching a crab. A crab happens when a rower can't remove the oar blade from the water at the finish of the drive (the part of the stroke where the rower is pulling), and a sloppy stroke occurs. This can happen when a rower loses grip of the handle, makes an error in judging when to remove or release the blade from the water, or if the boat tips to the side and there's nowhere for the rower to lower their hands to remove the blade. This usually means some timing problems for a few strokes. An over-the-head crab is even more serious. It's when the oar handle forces the rower onto his back and the handle goes over his head. This usually means the crew has to stop rowing, recover the oar, and then continue. I've even heard of people being choked by an oar, or having the oar handle get caught in a rower's stomach. The rower gets thrown out of the boat and the rest of the crew has to stop to get the rower back into the boat.

There is no time to think about all of that now, because it's time to row. The Black Oarsmen pick up the boat and walk towards the lake with the boat over our shoulders. We have our game faces on, and people stop what they're doing to see us row. I can see the interviewer watching us, and when I make eye contact he gives me a wink. I'm not sure if he is on our side or just thinks we're a joke.

When we place the boat down into the water, there are three other teams out there. More and more teams come over to watch, but I don't mind because I know we're something different to the rowing world. I'm also happy that no one in our boat has a lifejacket on. Ken isn't here with us, so I feel a little strange or alone, I guess. I brush the feeling aside.

We push off to the starting line and I tell myself, It's our time. The waves are strong, so it takes a little time to properly set up at the starting line. Preston is back in stroke seat, Malcolm is in seat three, I'm in two, and Alvin is in bow. I look over to size up our opponents, but Coach Jessica is ordering us to the catch. We reach forward as far as we can. I see that the other teams are at the finish, as if they just finished a stroke.

"Row!"

We take off. We are racing head to head with everyone. I can feel the boat moving as fast as it ever has. The waves are getting stronger, and the boat is rocking up and down with water splashing everywhere. Alvin starts screaming as he's rowing.

"There's water getting into the boat!"

"We're gonna flip," I yell to Coach Jessica.

"Keep going, don't stop this damn boat!"

Preston yells out that he's getting hit with waves, and we continue complaining while rowing. Coach Jessica is screaming her head off.

"My shorts are stuck to the seat," I yell out.

"Keep rowing, guys. This is it!"

In all the intensity, I am having trouble taking full strokes. My forearm is throbbing, there are blisters all over my hands, and the oar is slippery. There are no timeouts or breaks in rowing, so I bash on, taking extra care to make sure that my blade gets into the water at the same time as the others blades to avoid a crab. There is no more quit in me. I have felt pain all my life; it's my normal.

Two boats are ahead of us but not by much, and before I can figure out how we're doing we are across the finish line and in third place. We fold over our legs in exhaustion. Alvin taps my shoulder.

"We didn't get last!"

"I know."

"Not bad, guys," Coach Jessica says, "but could have been better. Now you see, Arshay, that's why you wear spandex, so your shorts won't get stuck."

All the guys agree that stuck or not, we're never wearing spandex, and she laughs and gives up.

We get off the boat and tip it up, and water comes pouring out. I'm not happy with our results, but I'm happy that we finished. I can't wait to see Ken and talk about setting team goals and how to become better. I am ready for a leadership role. The guys on the team always tease me, telling me to slow down, that I get too excited.

I know I get ahead of myself sometimes, so I decide to live my life the way I race on the boat and the erg.

It's all about drive and recovery.

PART 6
IOWA

My fifth-grade teacher, Mr. Fullerton, used to play us a song in class by Paper Lace called "The Night Chicago Died." The fictional song was about a shootout between Chicago Police and gangsters connected to Al Capone. The song talks about the silence in the city after many men were killed. I always heard how Chicago was a big gangster city in the days of Al Capone, and I know that same spirit of violence existed in Chicago when I was a kid. A few people were killed in our neighborhood each month, and every time we heard about it a piece of the neighborhood died too. We knew the people being killed, some more than others, and I could feel people's sadness when it would hit close to home. Kids wouldn't show up at school the next day. The outdoor basketball courts would be empty. Parents would keep their children inside, and the older guys from the block would disappear. It always seemed like a sign of war. The people being killed were a reflection of the West Side, and the West Side was a reflection of Chicago.

On the West Side, nobody was safe. The innocent bystander who worked for the city, the proud kid on the corner with "Chi Town" tattooed on his forearm, or the women that overdosed on drugs who'd been living off government assistance. Chicago was dying every time we turned on the news. I always wondered why this was happening in my city, my community, my block.

Little Fred, a cool older guy from my neighborhood who

the younger kids loved, always took the time to show me new moves on the basketball court. Little Fred was a breath of fresh air to us. He was shot and killed one day and our neighborhood died with him. Pastors tried their best to revive it with rallies. The gangs called for a war, and rumors were they knew who did it. They didn't tell the cops because they didn't believe it would be taken care of or didn't trust them to do it. So a war began that went on for years and killed many more people from many different neighborhoods.

As a kid, all the local stores sold the same cheap toys. There were cap guns to play cowboys and Indians, fake machine guns that made loud noises, and rubber knives to play cops and robbers. There were water guns to play war and shoot at strangers or to shoot at each other to keep us cool during the summer. When the street lights came on it was time to go inside, so we played with our stiff green army men and lined them up to shoot at each other. We had cheap toy wrestlers and cartoon heroes to fight each other until we fell asleep. If you were lucky, you had a Nintendo. It came with a gray and black gun that everyone wanted, and we felt tough when we held it and shot at the screen. Before you knew it, guns and fighting were considered cool and the violent movies we watched just added to it. By ten years old, everyone knew how to construct make-believe paper pistols. When we got older and the real thing became easy to find, they felt familiar in the guys' grip. On my block, you were respected for carrying a gun and criticized for carrying a book. I always hoped it would change because I didn't want other kids to grow up like me, never knowing what it's like to feel safe.

....

Ken knows the kind of trouble we can get into in our neighborhoods, so he has a plan to keep us safe for the summer and improve the way we think. He gets us a job at the Safe

Foundation, working and mentoring kids, knowing it will help us mature and change. Every day after work, we row or take entrepreneurship classes. On weekends, we go to the East Bank Club or chill at Ken and Jeni's place in the West Loop. We keep busy, and the daily activities and challenges keep our minds occupied.

One night over dinner at Ken and Jeni's place, we talk about the violence in Chicago.

"One of the main causes of violence in this city is because the community doesn't trust the Chicago Police Department," Jeni tells us. She talks about crooked cops, the innocent people in the correctional system, and the many kids that are beaten by the police. I know that not everyone is innocent because of what I've seen with my own eyes, and I do believe that there are some good cops out there; one works at our school. I also believe Jeni is on point because I think about Little Fred and how no one called the cops when he died. I believe that happens in every neighborhood.

I tell Jeni about what happened when I went to get Alvin the other morning.

"I was walking down his block and the cops pulled over and told me to come over to the car. When I got there, one cop opened my book bag, flipped it upside down, and poured everything out. When they saw I had nothing on me, they told me I was free to go." I was heartbroken, picking up all my books and paper. I know it's a crazy neighborhood and people have drugs and guns on them sometimes but it felt wrong.

"I told the cop, 'I hope you find who you looking for,' and he turned around said, 'What did you say?' He didn't say anything else. I think he could tell that I'm a good kid."

"I would've snapped," Malcolm said.

Preston gave him a look, "No you wouldn't."

"Don't ever talk back to the cops," Jeni warns us, "especially as young black men. Don't be intimidated, but be smart and do what they say. You won't win. That's a rule." We nodded, and I told the guys it might be better if we had local softball and basketball games for cops and the guys in the neighborhood to play together.

"Or if they came to block parties and school games to hang out, they might build some trust then."

"That will never happen," Alvin said, shaking his head. I know he's right. I've been getting stopped by police since I was a kid. No block party was going to change that.

"I do think that some cops would like to build a relationship with our community, but they get the sense that they're the enemy and hold back. And I guess we do think they're enemy, because we feel like the enemy, so it's just crazy. Remember when Ken dropped us off at Alvin's? The guys in the neighborhood thought we were riding with The People. It made us look like we can't be trusted."

"Exactly," Malcolm agreed, "being friends with cops will get us killed and cops being friends with us means problems from their boys."

When it comes time for us to head home, Ken gives us thirty dollars and puts us in a yellow cab. We get in the cab, and our eyes bug out when we see that the meter is already two dollars. Once we're around the corner, we have the cab driver let us out. He gets upset and tells us to get the hell out. We get out laughing, split the money four ways, and head towards the train.

I get off the train thinking about how crazy it is to live on the West Side of Chicago, watching my back as I walk to my house. I decide to sit on the porch when I get home, and a drug addict walks out of the hallway and asks for two bucks. I tell him no, and to stop doing drugs in the hallway. I can't wait to move out of this neighborhood, but it's all we can afford.

I think about the rules of the city, and how they are set by the different gangs. It's hard to believe that if I wear certain colors in the wrong neighborhood, I can get shot. If I wear my baseball hat slightly to the left or to the right in the wrong neighborhood, I can get shot. If I scratch my head and it looks like my fingers are making a certain gesture in the wrong neighborhood, I can get shot. What really drives me crazy is that I can't wear Converse shoes in my neighborhood, because the star symbol is a broken five-point star, and the five-point star represents the Vice Lords.

My neighborhood is called "Holy City" because every gang in it ends with the word Lord. There are Conservative Vice Lords, Traveler Vice Lords, Insane Vice Lords, Renegade Vice Lords, and Unknown Vice Lords. When the guys see one another they say, "What up, Lord?" I'm thankful for the places in the neighborhood that help kids stay off the street, like Family Focus, Better Boys Foundation, Urban Options, North Lawndale Center, Victory Outreach, and the Douglas Park Field House. There are local heroes that work to make Chicago better too. I hear certain names around like Father Pfleger, Bob Muzikowski, Craig Nash, Noel Castillo, Pastor Fernando Gonzales, Phil Jackson, Mike Trout, and Randy Brown. I head to bed with a burden in my heart and the city on my mind.

······················

Alvin, Malcolm, and I walk into entrepreneurship class on Western and Ogden Avenue and see at least twenty kids there from Urban Options. Ken is already there with Winnifred, and he asks one of the kids from the program to keep an eye on her. He talks to us about revenues and follows up with questions. When we answer correctly, he throws us a nutrition bar. Ken teases Malcolm a little bit because during our last class we brainstormed business ideas and Malcolm said we should take muffins and put frosting on them to sell.

"Fool, that's a cupcake," Alvin said. Ken couldn't stop laughing about it.

Towards the end of class, Ken takes out a five dollar bill and asks who wants it. Everyone starts calling out.

"I'll ask again, who wants this?"

Everyone just yells louder, raising their hands.

Ken screams, "Who wants this?"

Everyone screams louder until one student jumped up and grabbed the bill out of Ken's hands. He smiled.

"See? If you want it, you can't just yell and scream about it. You have to get up and go get it, period."

I'm inspired and pissed that I wasn't the one to jump up and get it, but now I know.

After class, Ken notices that Winnifred and the kid watching her aren't around, and he starts freaking out. He asks us to help him find Winnifred, so we jump up and start looking for them. Ten minutes pass, and there is no sign of either of them, so he calls the police. I've never seen him so rattled; he's shaking when he asks us all to go outside and search for them. Alvin wants to find the guy and beat him down.

The police show up and ask Ken a ton of questions. I'm worried about how Jeni is going to flip out on Ken once she shows up. She always comes to pick up Winnifred after class. I notice that Ken hasn't called her; he's mumbling to himself, "My wife is going to kill me."

I ask around to find out what the guy's name is, and one girl says it's "Q." We're all standing outside with Ken and the police when Q comes walking up carrying Winnifred like he's only been gone for two minutes. Ken runs towards him and grabs Winnifred and starts examining her. The police throw Q against the wall and he screams, "What happened?" You can tell the kid has no idea what is going on. Ken looks at Q's face and sees the same thing, so he asks the police to let him go.

Everything dies down. The police leave as Jeni pulls up in her black Mercedes-Benz bumping Biggie. Everyone tries to look normal. You can feel the awkward energy, and Jeni senses the tension in the air. Ken tries to keep a straight face as he says hello to her, but before she can say anything he hugs her and starts crying. He tells her what happened, and it's such a sad moment that we can only stand there and stare.

"It's okay," she says, hugging him back lightly. I'm not sure if Jeni is really okay or if she's going to let Ken have it once they get home. I can't help but think that Ken is good man, but he may trust people a little too much. I've heard Jeni yelling at him before about the people he's lent money too, people who have no intention of paying him back. It's a long list.

....

Coach Jessica calls me early on Saturday morning to tell me she will be late for practice. She asks me to start the team off with a mile run around the lagoon and some stretches.

Alvin, Preston, Malcolm, and I arrive at the boathouse and chat with Eugene, the caretaker. He asks what is new for the Black Oarsmen, and we shrug. I tell the guys we're supposed to run around the lagoon and start our stretches but of course they say they aren't doing that. I tell them Coach Jessica will be upset, but they don't care. It feels like one minute we are serious and the next we aren't. Alvin asks Eugene if we can all grab a kayak and row in the lagoon and he says, "Sure."

I've always been curious about the kayak. It is a narrow, banana-shaped boat with a double-bladed paddle. All the rich kids row them on the weekends at the lagoon. It seems pretty fun, and not too rigorous. We all grab one and head to the water, ignoring Coach Jessica's instructions. We race each other and it's fun, but still requires a lot of upper body strength. After ten minutes of being in the water, Malcolm picks up a dead fish from the lagoon with his paddle and tries tossing it in our kayaks. We all howl, grossed out by the stench. He hits Alvin with one, and it breaks into pieces against his life jacket. Alvin is not happy but continues to row as we laugh. We do another relay race in the kayaks and Malcolm and Alvin row in the area with the sail boats, even though it is prohibited. The area has some powerful waves, and Malcolm falls off of his kayak. We are cracking up until we remember he is a poor swimmer.

Alvin paddles over and sticks out his paddle to grab but Malcolm is flailing with panic and grabs the kayak instead. Now it looks like the kayak is about to flip over, so Alvin takes his paddle and starts pushing Malcolm away and telling him not to pull on the boat.

"Just chill, you have a life jacket on," I scream, though Malcolm doesn't seem to hear me. A man with a motor boat comes by and pulls him out of the drink. He looks legitimately nauseous in the other boat, but I can't stop laughing. The man delivers Malcolm safely to the dock and tells him to be careful and follow the rules. Eugene calls us over to tell us that Coach Jessica called and said she is not going to make it. She said we should just do some work on the erg and go home, but after what happened we decide to call it a day.

On the bus ride home, people are holding their noses because of Alvin's dead fish stink. It reminds me of cooking class when Chef Singleton said fish should smell like the ocean, not like fish. I feel bad for Alvin. We get off the bus together to hang out at his place.

When we get to his apartment, his big brother is there. I've never met him and Alvin has only spoken of him a few times. Alvin tells me he is a street salesman on the South Side who buys a new car every month. He looks as scary as Alvin's dad. He's rough looking with bloodshot eyes and scarred knuckles. He shouts to Alvin and tells him to come into the other room; it seems urgent so I hang back. I wonder what's going on.

Alvin comes back and tells me he has to go.

"What's up, man?"

"Something went down and I have to help my brother."

I shake my head. Alvin tears up until he turns around and leaves. I hear them get in his brother's car and drive off. His brother never looks at me once.

I think about what Alvin said on the bus in Philly. He said he'd only ever been in a fight to protect his family and friends. He said his dad told him he would end up in dead protecting love ones. It is exactly what has me worried.

I head home and chill, hoping that Alvin will call and tell me what happened. I pray Alvin will be smart. He is already considered intelligent. He's won chess competitions, he can hear a song three times and remember every word, he can solve any problem he learns in class, and he's a good reader. To me, smart is more than just understanding puzzles, remembering words, or quoting facts. To me, smart is being able to stay out of trouble, knowing when to shut your mouth, being open to learning, hanging out with the right crowd, and thinking of consequences before every action. Ken and I both had faith that Alvin is changing, and now I'm worried.

He calls a few hours later and doesn't sound good.

"What's wrong? What happened?"

"Man, I feel so bad. The guy my brother is working with messed up his money, and he wanted me to help jump him. Man, that's not me anymore."

"So what happened?"

"My brother went to his house and rang the doorbell, and the guy came out talking crazy. I ran up and started hitting him with a pool stick."

"God, Alvin."

"What do I do? It's my brother. I don't feel right. How am I going to hit someone with a pool stick, then go to work Monday and help kids?"

"Listen, there was a time when you would beat someone up and you didn't care or feel bad. Now you do. You are changing, man. This life isn't for you anymore."

I tell him he has to come to church with me, and he says he will...soon. We hang up the phone, and my heart is heavy for him. At the same time, I'm angry. I'm angry about where we live and how we're growing up. I'm angry that the odds are always stacked against us, so everything is a struggle. I'm jealous of the guys we race because the odds are with them. I wonder if it makes rowing, and life, easier for them.

....

It's the end of summer in 1998, and we've all survived. Most of the guys spent their time working. I took the month of August off from rowing and traveled with the Victory Outreach Church Drama Team. I joined because I wanted to stay busy and focus because there is no rowing. We traveled to most inner city churches in the Midwest and helped their communities by putting on a play called Last Chance that portrayed the life of gang members, drug addicts, and broken families. The play was very powerful and relatable. Many young people saw themselves through the violence of the play and asked afterwards what they could do to change and get out of the gang life. I was honored to be a part of that this summer, and witness so many people change. There is a saying that your life becomes better by making others' lives better, and it's true to me.

I learned a lot about myself during that trip with Victory Outreach. Seems like road trips and not having any cash brings you face to face with who you really are. I didn't know I had a problem with humility and my attitude until this road trip.

Pastor Fernando would ask me all the time, "Are you happy?"

"Yeah," I always answered.

"Well, let your face know it!"

His leadership style is tough love, different from Ken's style, but I know I need both. Once, while we were traveling, the pastor sat me down and told me I let people control me.

"Yeah, but—,"

"See? Stop and listen." Pastor got on me all summer for never stopping at "yeah." It was always, "Yeah, but..." with me.

"Anytime you're laughing and smiling and having a great day, someone knows they can say something to ruin your smile and control you. Don't let that take place, my friend. Just roll with the punches and keep moving."

....

The minute I arrive back in Chicago, the first number I call is Ken's.

"What's up, buddy? How was your summer?"

"Perfect, we should all get together."

"Sure. I have good news to share with you guys anyway. Come over for lunch tomorrow."

Malcolm and Alvin say they're coming, but Preston says he can't make it. I feel like we are growing apart. I'm not sure if it's in my head, or if I'm too lame for him now, or because I've heard he's smoking a lot of pot and doesn't want to be around.

In the morning, the three of us meet at Ken's place, and we're all happy to catch up and talk about the summer. We thank him for the summer job. I notice that he has a huge painting on the wall of us rowing in the Lagoon, and Ken tells us Jeni got it for him for his birthday.

"This is nice," Malcolm says, "but they're black faces with white face features."

Alvin starts laughing and I tell them to shut up about it. I ask Ken what the good news is, and he says he'll tell us later.

"Jeni and I are going to take you guys to Manny's for lunch."

"Jeni is really coming?"

"Yeah, why? Surprised?" Ken says sarcastically.

We're excited because we love when Jeni hangs out. She's just so real and understands the world like we do. Ken and Jeni get Winnifred ready, and we head to the garage to Jeni's car. She puts Winnifred in the car seat and then heads to the driver seat, while Ken walks over to shotgun. We quickly realize with the car seat the three of us can't fit in back.

Jeni suggests, "I will sit on Ken's lap, and Alvin can drive."

"No," Ken cuts her off. "There is no way Alvin is driving the brand new Mercedes."

"He has a driver's license."

"No way. We can get a cab too."

"Ken, that's ridiculous," Jeni says, annoyed. "You know what, fine. Ken, you drive. I will sit on Alvin's lap; we're going less than a mile." Alvin is smirking as he all but skips over to the passenger side.

"You know what, Alvin, you drive." Ken tosses him the keys. Everyone in the car cracks up except Ken.

We pull up in front of Manny's and Ken praises Alvin for doing a good job of getting us there in one piece. We laughed at all the funny looks we got while Alvin drove: leaned back, bumping Biggie in the Mercedes, with Jeni and Ken in passenger seat and two black dudes in back playing with a little white baby. I'm sure it was confusing.

The mostly-empty restaurant is set up like an old school cafeteria. Alvin and I take our time trying to choose between the fish and baked chicken. I can feel eyes on me and notice a white woman behind me looking irritated. She sighs and cuts in line in front of us.

"Excuse me," Jeni says, staring the woman down, "get back behind them."

"Excuse me? Who in the hell are you talking too?" the lady snaps back, shocking all of us.

"You jumped in front of them, so get back behind them."

The lady's husband comes over and tells Jeni to calm down. We watch in stunned disbelief. Jeni tells the husband, "No, you calm down."

The man grabs his wife, "Let's get behind them, this women is a total ass." Ken interjects and tells the guy not to talk to Jeni like that. The situation feels like it's getting out of hand.

"Hey, guys," I try to step in, "it's okay."

The guy grabs his wife by the hand, and they turn around and leave.

After they're gone, Ken asks Jeni what happened. She explains that the lady threw a fit and jumped in front of us in line.

"Don't ever be intimidated," she says and walks away.

"White people, man," Malcolm whispers.

We get our food, head to the table, and everyone starts laughing and eating. I want to thank Jeni, but I can tell that Ken doesn't want to talk about it anymore.

After lunch, we drop Malcolm and Alvin off on Kedzie and Van Buren near Alvin's place, and I decide to hang out with Ken and Jeni for a while longer. We drive south on Kedzie, and as we turn onto Harrison, I hear the tires of a car making a sharp turn. Behind us now is a black Crown Victoria police car; I see the cops inside looking directly at me. I tell Jeni we're about to get pulled over, but Ken tells me to relax.

They hit the sirens.

The police jump out and head to the front of the Mercedes. As soon as they realize who is in the front seats, you can see the look of surprise on their faces. I'm sure we got pulled over because only drug dealers in Alvin's neighborhood drive Mercedes. The officer approaches the driver's side, and Jeni rolls the window down.

"What's the problem?"

"You rolled a left turn in front of me. You should have slowed down."

"That's BS; you were a block away. It's obvious why you pulled us over."

The cop is seething. He tells Ken he should calm her down before he locks her up.

"Calm down, Jeni."

"No, Ken. You saw that they were a block away." Jeni turns back to the cop. "You gonna give me a ticket? Do it now and don't waste my time."

The cop backs up. "Next time, drive carefully."

He tells Jeni she can leave, and by the look on his face he realizes he went too far. I don't think that cop had any idea he was running into the wrong people.

It's a quiet ride back to their house, and I start thinking about the differences and similarities between Ken and Jeni. I know Ken was raised in New Jersey with two siblings; his mother is a teacher and his dad an orthodontist. Ken went to an Ivy League college and majored in Science and Economics. He was a great rower and quick thinker. He moved to Chicago and made his first million in his twenties. He's a born entrepreneur and always had a heart to make a difference in the inner city. Jeni was born in Indiana with two siblings; her mother was a nurse and her dad a doctor. Her parents are divorced. Jeni went to school for music, sang opera, and was the runner-up for Miss Indiana. She realized there was a need for good criminal defense attorneys and decided to go to law school.

Ken and Jeni met at a bar and hit it off, had Winifred, and got married. I don't think they are a "single soul dwelling in two bodies" or have the chemistry of Cliff and Claire Huxtable, but they see the world the same way. They both embody the importance of working hard to have wealth, good health, friendship, family, love, and having more than enough to give. Alvin told me he thinks they both decided to get wealthy just so they had more to give. I admire their choice to live a selfless life because I've grown up around takers all my life. I think my first word was "mine." Being around Ken, Jeni, and my post-Victory Outreach mom, I feel surrounded by givers, and it's making my heart change. I'm torn between wanting to be a chef and wanting to help others.

When we get to Ken and Jen's place, I ask Ken what the good news is that he mentioned earlier.

"I totally forgot because of the craziness today!" He disappears upstairs and comes back with a paper from the Pennsylvania Gazette.

"It's about the rowing team."

"Another article to put on the wall?" I'm excited. It an alumni profile about Ken and his efforts called "Sculling for Success."

I shake Ken's hand.

"This is awesome, man." I tell him that I want to be captain, because I was ready to lead the team and I knew there were more headlines to come.

"You got it, buddy."

"I'm glad Manley said yes. I didn't know that the team cost 25,000 dollars."

"It's expensive, but you don't need to worry about that."

I start to ask him how big the check was for the woman with the car, but he laughs and cuts me off before I can finish. I start laughing too, and deep down I know that I will never get it out of him.

I'm excited to be back to school on the first day. Some of the guys on the team are wearing our black Manley Crew hoodies to represent. I love how it is written, in red with red oars framing the top and bottom.

Alvin and I have second period African American History

class together with my favorite teacher, Mr. Deligiannis. Mr. D. knows how to do his job and make it interesting; some of the other teachers just do a job.

After second period, Alvin and I run into Pookie G., Malcolm's cousin.

"Pookie G.," Alvin laughs, "the guy who throws skittles at buses."

Pookie just smiles.

"What 'sup, German boy? Did you transfer here?"

"I want to be on the rowing team. Philly was fun."

"You can't be shy here, boy," Alvin teases. Pookie laughs. I tell him practice starts next week and that I will see him then. Coach Jessica and Ken want us to spend the week recruiting new students for the team, so we talk to students in the hall and post flyers. The energy in the school seems more vibrant than ever. Both the football and basketball teams are expected to excel this year. Craig Nash has been hired to help and grow the school. Nash is known in the community for his positive energy and mentoring.

There's a program at school called Umoja, founded by a woman named Lila Leff. I had never heard the word "college" used so much until she decided to bring this program to Manley. The focus is to create a family-school-community partnership to affect positive changes in the lives of Manley students. Lila's passion is contagious. I'm excited about the school year.

A few days after it starts, I finally have a chance to catch up with Grace and walk her to the bus stop. She tells me she spent her summer working. I know her mom is a single parent and mother of three so Grace works to help her out. She is sweet to give up her summer to help provide, and that's just another reason why I like her.

I'm nervous walking her to the bus stop because I don't want to be late for my first team meeting as captain. It's important for me to be on time, so I'm hoping the bus will hurry up and whisk Grace away. When it comes, I hug her and sprint back to the school and head right to the gym. The door is closed, and there is a note that says we are meeting in Room 108.

I rush to the room, and there are already a dozen people inside.

"Look who decided to show up," Coach Jessica teases.

"I was in the cooking room," I tell her, wiping the sweat from my head. Alvin looks at me and shakes his head.

"It will just be a meeting today," Coach Jessica starts, but she waits a few minutes for others to show up. She steps out in the hallway, and we commence talking. I hear a loud raspy voice that sounds like Chris Tucker coming from the hallway.

"Guess who's coming over tonight?"

"Who?" someone asks.

"These nuts," he yells back, walking into the classroom. He is tall, dark, and skinny, with nappy hair and a big birthmark on the right side of his temple. "What 'sup niggas and niggettes?"

Everyone is laughing. I decide to make my presence known because I'm the captain.

"What 'sup, my brother?"

He looks over at me, scanning from my shoes to my head as if I shouldn't have spoken to him.

"You not my brotha until you've drunk suga water."

Alvin looks confused. "You mean sugar water?"

"No, I mean suga water."

Alvin asks if he's some kind of comedian or something, but I tell him it's cool. Everyone is laughing at this guy or laughing with him. I'm not sure.

"Man," I tell him, "I've had plenty of suga water."

"Not Kool-Aid, just water and suga."

I nod. "With every meal."

"The black kid struggle," he says, reaching for my hand. "I guess you my brotha."

I shake his hand and instantly feel a connection.

"Dude," Alvin says in disbelief, "you just drunk straight sugar in water?"

"Yeah, man, all the time. You have to try it."

"Hell to the naw."

I look back at the kid, and he is already cracking jokes to some girl. I tell him my name is Arshay and that I'm the team captain.

"I'm Josh, and who made you captain?"

Everyone laughs again, and I'm hoping he isn't another Malcolm.

Coach Jessica comes in, and I notice that Preston and Malcolm aren't there. Coach Jessica asks me, but I tell her I don't know.

"Okay, guys, listen up. First thing: Coach Victor is no longer with us."

I'm not surprised. I didn't think he was going to stick around; some of the guys were a real pain in the butt last year.

"For those who are new, we row in a sport called crew. It's pretty much always been a white sport, but you guys add something new and fresh."

Josh says, "Like flavor."

"There are a few people here from last year's team who raced and did well. Arshay, our new captain, would like to talk about that?"

Everyone turns to look at me.

"Yes, rowing is unique to me. There are days when you feel like it's your time, like the best of your talents is just about to materialize, that you're on the verge of history. Then there are days when you feel like you don't belong and you should do everyone a favor and crawl back into your mom's womb. The good news is you change for the better."

"I've changed," Alvin nods.

Elliot jumps in, "Me too."

Everyone starts clapping, and I feel amazing after speaking. I want to make a difference; I feel like it's our year. All I know is the water is my peace. I live in a place where I have been taught not to swim in deep water, to always wear a life jacket when I'm in a boat. I feared the water and any sport that had to do with water. Now, when I'm in the boat, I don't hear gunshots or ambulance sirens. I don't see gang signs, and I don't have fear because Alvin is behind me and Preston is in front of me. I feel powerful.

Coach Jessica talks to us about upcoming plans and an upcoming race in Iowa. Josh expresses how much he wants to go to that one. She also tells us that they are looking for a new coach and it is posted all over Rowing News Magazine. When we are dismissed, Josh jumps up.

"See you fools later, and don't let the bed bugs bite."

We can't believe he really said that. Coach Jessica suggests to me after the meeting that I should pay a visit to Preston and Malcolm and see if they are going to row this year.

When I leave the school building, I see a few of the ex-ball players from Manley hanging out on the corner. They all look awful. Only a few years ago these guys were star athletes making the local paper, with real potential to get into a good college. They are probably only about twenty years old, but they look forty. Their clothes are too big, hair is uncombed, eyes are bloodshot, and their lips are darkened from smoking blunts. My heart bleeds for them, and it bothers me because some of the ball players in my class are heading down the same road.

I blame some of the teachers and coaches for this. It seems like the only responsibility the basketball players have is to give 100 percent when it comes to winning. Everything else is given to them. They are given good grades, nice shoes, girls, special attention, and protection. Guys like me have to earn all of that. Maybe that's a good thing, because the players that aren't good enough to get scholarships seem to fall apart. When you work extra hard through high school and earn every grade, it's easier to resist the nonsense of the streets. I feel like the coaches develop them too much as an athlete but not as a human being. It was almost as if existence was about basketball skills and not life skills. I realize now why all the traveling, classes, mentoring, and exposure were more of a priority than rowing. If this program was shut down, I'd know exactly what I'd want to do next.

....

I take the bus over to Preston's and feel nervous walking into the old neighborhood. Michelle opens the door and greets me with a big hug.

"Where you been, boy?"

"Staying out of trouble."

"That's good. Preston is in back."

I walk into Preston's room, and he's ironing his clothes.

"Coop! What 'sup, nigga?"

"Hey, man, what happened to school and row practice?"

"Listen, man, I'm tryna make this money."

"Me too, that's why I'm doing this row thing."

He laughs. "Listen, Coop, you do you and I'm going to do me." I tell him how much we need him in school and on the team, and he promises he will be there tomorrow.

"Donald's coming over and my boy Big C is picking us up. Ride with us."

I shake my head, "No, man, it's okay. I'm going home."

"Man, be a friend, not a captain."

"Okay, man, I will chill with you for a bit."

He asks me about Grace.

"You know better than me man."

"Dude, you need better. She's not right keeping my nigga waiting." I lie in his bed and ask him to change the subject.

When the other guys show up we hop into their car; I'm happy to see Donald. We laugh about old times. Big C is a big, brown dude with shady eyes. He keeps looking at me through the rearview mirror. He pulls over and takes out a blunt.

"Coop, you smoke weed?"

"Naw, I'm too young."

"Well, you will today. It's gonna make you feel good."

I look at him. "I don't smoke."

They all try to get me to smoke, and I tell them that weed will kill my brain cells.

"Come on, man, with that."

"It calms us down," Preston pipes in, "and plus I remember everything."

I say to Big C, "You know anyone on cocaine?"

"Yeah, plenty."

"What's the first drug they smoked?"

He rolls his eyes. "Man, just shut up and get high off this contact."

I say, "I'm out," and get out of the car. I tell Preston he knows where to find me.

At this moment, walking to the train, I know that what Preston and I have now will just be a memory. I am sold on the vision that Ken, Chef Singleton, the Pastor, and my mom have for me: becoming a great chef, rower, leader, speaker, and entrepreneur. I am willing to be called lame, cut off old friends, and give up fun times and parties to do so.

I call Ken when I get home and tell him that I don't think Preston is going to continue to row, and that we need more direction as a team. He tells me to come by his office tomorrow so we can talk about it. I feel bad bothering him about the rowing team when he has a million-dollar company to run. I know that there are days he loses hundreds of thousands of dollars and freaks out. I never want to catch him on those days.

....

After talking to my fifth-period teacher, I walk past a class-room and see a friend of mine. I yell hello and wave. Mr. Edwards, a Physics teacher from the Caribbean, jumps up.

"Don't interrupt my class."

"Okay, chill!" He gets in my face, and everyone is look-ing. I don't want to seem like a punk, so I walk away and say, "Screw you."

"Say it again! Come on, say it again."

Everyone is laughing and saying I'm getting punked, but I keep my mouth shut and walk back to my class. I think he might jack me up. I sit down, and everyone is trying to egg me on to say something more. I don't and they laugh. I feel bad because I know it's my fault and I shouldn't have said what I said. I failed myself because I know once I became a captain I've lost the privilege to blow up, explode, talk back, or say things like that to teachers. I say privilege because it feels good to do those things, but I know people are looking up to me and I have to be an example. I sit in my chair, angry and embarrassed. My friend Deyki keeps saying that Mr. Edwards is going to tap my butt. I say nothing. I think about how hard it is to stay clean in a dirty environment.

After fifth period, Mr. Edwards comes to my class and walks up to me.

"What's your name?"

"Arshay."

He hands me a piece of paper. "Here is my address. I am having students over this Saturday morning at ten a.m. Be there."

I wonder what the hell is going on. I think he may try to kill me. I've felt like I was going to die so many times before and been fine, so maybe I will go. I ball the paper up and put it in my pocket. I walk down the hallway and hear Josh with his raspy voice. I see him over by the stairs, telling jokes to an audience. He is magnetic. I have to get him alone and try to sell him on becoming a rower.

I walk over and poke his back, and he turns around like he's about to strike.

"Boy, get your paws off me." I laugh, and he squints at me. "Do I know you?"

"Come on, man, you know me."

"You been eating Cheetos?"

Everyone starts laughing, and I say, "Dude, my breath don't smell. Listen, man, we're going on the water tomorrow to row, we can really use you."

"Use me? Only women can use me."

I'm frustrated because he won't stop joking, so I just nod at him and walk away.

"Arshay," I turn around to hear him out, "see you tomorrow."

"Cool."

I can tell Josh is the kind of guy who will clown you so bad you will want to hide in a closet. I have no doubt in my mind he will be a comedian.

After school, I see Alvin and ask if he wants to go Ken's office with me. He says no and asks if I've noticed he's been limping. I haven't.

"What happened?"

"I have a hernia. I need surgery."

"No, man! We have a race in a few weeks in Iowa."

He tells me he can't row, and I can't help but think about how things are falling apart. No Preston, No Malcolm, and now no Alvin. He tells me he will be back before I know it, but I feel like every time we're about to fly, gravity comes and pulls us down. I think about what Ken said the first time he spoke when he told us rowing isn't for everybody. My mind starts playing tricks on me, so I quickly snap out of it and run upstairs to talk to another friend, Dwayne Banks, about joining the rowing team.

Dwayne is a light-skinned, skinny kid who can sing his butt off. All he seems to care about is singing. He has a good heart and is nice to everyone, so I want him in. I explain the rowing program to him, and he tells me he will fill in until Alvin comes back. It is pretty strange to hear that because Alvin and his gang chased these guys freshmen year to give them a beat down. I realize being a captain takes loads of responsibility, and it's my job to take some of the load off the coaches.

I get to Ken's office, and everyone looks really busy and acts like they don't see me. There are computer screens everywhere with thousands of numbers on them. It makes me think of the movie Trading Places with Eddie Murphy. People are screaming and shouting curse words like crazy. I know Ken is a trader, but I don't really understand what that means.

When I see Ken, he introduces me to everyone. Most are nice, and a few others are a little confused. Ken tells me he wants me to sit in on a meeting with him.

"What meeting?"

"Just a bunch of jag-offs asking for money."

"What do you mean asking for money?"

He tells me they want him to invest in their project, and I tell him I will sit in.

Ken gives me his credit card and asks me to run down to the ATM before the meeting to get $200. He never has cash. I tell him I've never used an ATM before, but he says I can figure it out. When I get to the machine, I figure it out pretty fast. After I get the $200, the machine asks if I would like to take more money out. The little devil on my shoulder is chanting, "Do it, do it," and I know he'd never know. Luckily there is a little angel on my right shoulder that tells me I shouldn't.

I can't even believe that thought occurred to me; it feels dirty. When I get the receipt, I'm shocked. I've never seen that many zeroes before.

I head back up and give Ken the money, and we go into the meeting. There are two white men with suits on that are looking at me like I'm a joke.

Ken informs them, "Arshay here is my ears, so let's hear it." I don't really understand what's going on in the meeting, but I know I want to attend more so I can understand.

Ken decides to drive me home. While we drive, he explains trading to me and how he thinks drug dealers would make good traders because they're leaders, take risks, and make quick decisions.

"If you play video games and are good with math, you can be a good trader."

He asks if I want to learn, but I tell him that I want to cook or work with youth.

"Cool. Did you look at any cooking schools for college?"

"Yes, I looked into Johnson and Wells, Cooking Institute of America, Cooking Hospitality Institute of Chicago, and Cornell University. They have a hotel management program."

Ken looks at me. "Cornell also has rowing."

"That sounds cool."

I tell him that Chef Singleton wants me to work for free on Fridays cooking at the Hilton O'Hare.

"An internship is awesome for you. Trust me, it will be a good payoff."

"Yes, but the idea of working for free is crazy. I can work and make cash."

"Work for free, trust me." I tell him okay, and tell him about the full schedule Chef Singleton has set me up with this year.

"Like what?"

"Serve at the Mayor's dinner, work at the chocolate factory, and cook at the Palmer House Hilton." Ken tells me that Manley is doing a good job of getting me out there, and now I have to stay committed.

"When you're done with cooking school and college I will hook you up with my sister-in-law Nicole's boyfriend, Rick. He's one of the owners of one of the best restaurants in Chicago. It's called Blackbird and the kitchen is run by Chef Paul Kahan." I tell him I don't know who that is, but it sounds amazing.

Ken asks me what the line-up is for the Iowa race. I tell him I'm thinking Pookie G. as coxswain. Ken is shocked by that because Pookie G. never talks, but I think he will.

"I will row stroke seat, and this new guy Dwayne in three seat for Alvin, because Alvin has a hernia. There's also this new kid, Josh. You'll love him. He is one of the funniest dudes I know, but you can't tell him that. He will row two seat. Elliot will be in bow."

Ken thanks me and tells me Coach Jessica let him know that I've been taking on a leadership role.

"Yeah, but I've been reading this book on leadership that's been helping me. I feel like we need more of a direction."

Ken asks where I got the book, and I tell him that a guy at church gave me twenty bucks to read it.

"That's awesome. I'll find a new coach to kick your butts." I thank him and tell him he should come to church with me sometime.

"Maybe not."

"Why?"

"I don't have a problem with Jesus. I just have a problem with his people." I tell him I've never heard that before and we both laugh.

When I get home, my mom is sleeping on the couch with her Bible on her chest. I'm so proud of her. She's working at a nursing job with my aunt and is busy all the time now.

She's given me the freedom to allow Ken and Jeni to be like a second family to me. It's different for Alvin because his dad doesn't really trust white people, which I'm sure comes from his personal experience.

My personal experience is this: one time, a white cop stopped me and made a fool out of me on the street, and one time a black man stopped me in middle school and said I wouldn't amount to anything and predicted I would die before I turned eighteen. Years later, a white man offered me an opportunity to row and taught me everything he knows, and a black man gave me a job and inspired my poetry. There are good people and there are bad people, the lost and the found. I am thankful that my mother is open to new learning.

....

That Saturday, I head to Mr. Edward's house. I'm curious to know what he wants with me. I'm a little fearful, but I don't pass up an opportunity or challenge. I'm thinking he has two pairs of boxing gloves in his backyard and wants to settle everything outside the school. I have heard of him fighting a student before. I knock on the door, and he opens it and invites me in. He looks at me and smiles, and I give a fake smile back.

I step inside, and there are beautiful chandeliers every-where. I see pictures of beautiful Caribbean kids on the wall. I follow him to the back, and there are a bunch of students from Manley that I've never spoken to. Mr. Edwards offers me pizza and a soda. He can tell that I'm confused, but he doesn't say anything, just smiles. I have to pinch myself because it has to be a dream.

"Listen up, guys," Mr. Edwards says to the group, "Welcome to our first Academic Decathlon training."

I've seen this competition on TV before. It's an academic competition for high schools every year that has extremely hard math, art, economics, and science questions.

"I chose you guys because you all have the highest grade point averages in Manley."

I'm confused because I know plenty of students who have a higher grade point average than me and they aren't here.

"Mr. Cooper and I had a run in during class this week, and something in his eyes told me to invite him here," he looks over at me. "We'd love for you to be a part of this if you'd like."

I thank him as I smile and nod at him. I don't feel smart enough to be in this program, but I'm willing to take the challenge.

Afterward, I sit with Mr. Edwards and discuss my schedule and leadership role with the rowing team, and it turns out it won't work out for me to join the decathlon team. I thank him for the opportunity and apologize for my actions earlier in the week. Mr. Edwards tells me that I'm a good kid, and I tell him he's a good man. We say our goodbyes, and I leave, happy to know there is another teacher out there who can turn a bad situation into an opportunity.

....

A few weeks later, I find myself in the corn fields of Iowa with nothing around. This state has horror movie potential.

I have confidence in the guys I am racing with, although it is weird rowing without Preston, Malcolm, and Alvin. Malcolm disappeared and started doing his own thing. Teammates seldom have any clue about the effect it has on you when they quit a team, get suspended, or get injured. Everything becomes heavier.

It is a quiet ride to the lake in Coach Jessica's truck. Josh is growing on us and keeps us laughing, but he never says much about his personal life. When I bring up family, he changes the subject.

Dwayne has caught on to rowing pretty quickly and tells me that it's by far the hardest sport he's done in his life. Pookie G. has been talking a little more and spends a lot of time with me and Alvin while he's recovering. Pookie G. is super smart and has a lovely mother that believes I will be rich one day. Every time she sees me she asks when I'm going to buy her a house.

Elliot is a senior now and still really laid back. He is just so humble and does whatever he is told. He tells us that this team changed his life. He says crew keeps him sane.

As we pull up to the race, Josh asks where our boat is, and Coach Jessica tells us we will share someone else's boat. The beautiful thing about crew culture is that they share equipment with each other. Josh asks if they know we're black, and Coach Jessica laughs.

"We will see."

"And not Carlton black," Josh says, "Wesley Snipes black."

We crack up.

"Okay, guys," Coach Jessica tells us, "I'm going to check on equipment, so just hang out and stay close."

Josh jumps out of the car and starts scoping out all the ladies with pink toes, and I tell him to keep it cool. He tells me I need to chill and enjoy being a teenager, but it's race time.

"Dude," Josh says to me, "before we race, we should come out like the Chicago Bulls. We can bebop the theme song. 'From North Lawndale, rowing in stroke seat, Arshay Cooperrrrr.'"

I start laughing and tell him it's not a bad idea. It is a different vibe than the other races. At most races, people just stare at us, but at this one it seems like they don't want us there. The staff isn't as nice to us as they were at previous races, so we stay to ourselves. Pookie G. senses it too and tells me to look at Josh. I look over and Josh is throwing pennies into the crowd, but they can't see where they're coming from. I walk towards Josh to tell him to stop.

"It's those damn black guys," someone screams.

Josh balls up a fist. "You hear what they just said about us?"

"Dude," I tell him, "it is those damn black guys. Chill the hell out, man."

We walk off without looking.

I see Coach Jessica walking towards us urgently, and I think we're in trouble.

"Guys, our race is starting now. There was some miscommunication." She tells us we are racing in a head race, which means boats begin with a rolling start at intervals of ten to twenty seconds and are timed over a set distance.

"The race is 5000 meters," she tells us, "and you have to row 2000 meters out of the start and you may not have time to rest." I ask her if we have to sprint to the start. "Yes, because you guys are starting late."

I'm not happy about that, but we get the boat, walk it to the dock, and quickly jump in. We start rowing to the start line, saying every curse in the book.

"You think they're cheating us?" Josh asked.

"Maybe," Elliot says, but I just row. I angrily tell Pookie G. that he has to motivate us and give us something.

"Row lightly." I give up on him and try to motivate them myself, but the boat is not well balanced.

"Port, raise your oar, and starboard, lower yours," I scream, and the boat balances.

Boats are flying off the start line as we pull up; the staff in the motor boat tells us we need to quickly turn and go because all seven of the boats are already gone.

"We just got here, can we get a break?" I ask, but they tell me no, we need to turn now and row. It is brutal. My hands are starting to bleed, my back is hurting, and I know it is going to be all heart. We are driving back with all our strength, and I feel the boat moving. The race is so long, and there's nobody else in sight. Out of nowhere, Pookie G. starts screaming.

"Okay, fools, let's do this." We are all in shock.

"Power ten strokes in two," he screams, "One, two, now!"

He counts down with each stroke and is shouting at us, telling us we got this. He is saying anything that comes to mind and cursing like crazy. It's funny, but at the same time it is working.

We finally pass the finish line, feeling half past dead. We lean back on each other laps. When we get off the boat, Coach Jessica is smiling.

"You boys just became men."

We can't say a word, we are so tired.

"You guys basically sprinted over four miles straight; that's impressive. You guys raced all college teams from Iowa and came in last by two seconds, and that's only because of that 2000 meter pre-race sprint that shouldn't have happened. I'm sorry about that. I believe you could have placed first."

Coach Jessica heads off to wrap things up, and we're in the parking lot laughing and repeating some of the stuff Pookie G. was saying. In the parking lot, a white kid jumps out of a gray minivan and slams the door.

"No, mom, you listen to me! This is my event, not yours." The poor mom is trying to calm him down.

"No, mom, you calm down."

Pookie G. starts laughing a bit, but Josh tells him it isn't funny and starts walking towards the kid. I grab Josh, and he pushes my hands away. Josh grabs the kid arm.

"Apologize to your mom."

The kid is visibly freaked out.

"Who the hell are you? Who the hell are you?"

The kid has to be about sixteen. The mother jumps out of the car.

"Leave my son alone," she screams.

Josh raises his hands in the air.

"Listen, man, you need to apologize to your mother. If I talked to my mom like that, she would bust my head, but I don't have her like that. You have yours. I'm just saying, I will take your mom if you don't want her."

The kid looks down, embarrassed.

"Mom, let's talk in the car." He doesn't say anything else to Josh. He just gets in the car.

The mom gives Josh a slight nod and a small smile and gets into the car.

"I have my problems," Josh says, "but I can't take men disrespecting their moms."

"Yeah," I tell him, "that would have been a stick upside my head."

I don't know anything about Josh's history, but I like him a lot. I want to keep him close and teach him everything I've learned from my mentors. I feel like he is just what we need to complete our team.

PART 7
NORTHWESTERN
UNIVERSITY

Winter in Chicago feels like a pair of windshield wipers, slapping you from side to side for four months straight. It's December, so I know it's just beginning, but I already see people walking backwards in the street because the wind is so strong it stings their faces. Some tall buildings have large, sharp icicles hanging off the roof, so the city blocks off a lot of the sidewalks. Public transportation is overcrowded because so many cars have frozen gas tanks. I see neighbors arguing in the street over a bucket. We get so much snow that it can take hours to shovel out a parking spot, only to have a neighbor steal it from you the minute it's clear. Up and down the streets of the city, there are buckets, chairs, and traffic cones "saving" freshly shoveled parking spots for people when they leave for work. Some people respect the saved spots, but when someone doesn't, there is almost always a fight.

In spite of the freezing cold, I've learned to find beauty in the city. I've been on Christmas break for the last few days, so I'm using the money I've saved to explore. In my sixteen years of living, I have never had a teacher, family member, or friend tell me to go and get lost in the city I was born and raised in. I have dreams of traveling and exploring other cities and countries, but how can I if I've never seen the four corners of my own?

I fall in love walking down State Street; it is so beautiful. Christmas music is playing in front of Marshall Field's and people look so happy coming in and out of the building. Even the street preacher in front of Old Navy looks happy telling everyone that they are condemned to hell. I walk past Daley Plaza, and there is a huge Christmas tree with people singing in front; pictures are being taken of Baby Jesus and the angels. I walk into the Borders bookstore and have never seen so many books in my life. I'm amazed at the amount of young people that are there sitting on the floor, just to read. Across the street from Borders is the Chicago Theater. I am too scared to walk inside; it looks so fancy, so I just stare through the window. I walk over to Michigan Avenue, and it's filled with people with shopping bags. I stare up at the Wrigley Building, which reminds me of Gotham City. It looks like an old castle, unbreakable. I stick around and admire the Chicago street talent, the kids beating buckets with their drumsticks, the saxophone players, the singers out in the cold hustling for change. I take a bus to Hyde Park and check out the huge houses that leave me in awe. I also find beauty in the inner city of Chicago, like the talented old men on Madison Street who sings in front of garbage cans full of burning wood to keep warm. They sound flawless. I admire the kids on the West Side who shovel snow off the outdoor basketball court to play ball. Even the cold can't keep them from being dedicated to their sport.

The Christmas lights on Homan and Flournoy Street are amazing. What the community does with that block during the holidays is better than any Christmas decorations I've seen on TV. It's nice to see churches get together and give cheerfully to the homeless, and see community centers put on creative holiday events. The brotherhood at barbershops and the positive image they give young kids is never talked about, but those guys deserve an award, especially my barber Dee.

I have a reality check, because my head is so filled with negativity from what the media shows me and what I hear on the radio about gangs, drug dealers, corrupt politicians, crooked cops, city segregation, and poor public schools. I know these things shouldn't be ignored, but I'm ready to hear about solutions and not just the problems. At one time, I believed that there was no good left in Chicago, and this exploration has reminded me of all of its beauty, culture, and goodness.

My mom and I finish wrapping some Christmas gifts, and I think back to the times when we didn't have Christmas. To see us now is amazing. My mom is always dancing around because she's been seeing one of the leaders from the church. His name is Keith, and he's a great musician. He is the same guy who pays kids to read different books. Now that I think about it, I am probably the only kid he's paid. My brother Shaundell is expected to come and have Christmas dinner with us, so that is good news for everyone. Last time I saw him was in the hospital a couple months ago. He was there because a drug addict picked up a broken bottle and sliced his face open after an argument. He's been living with his baby mama and seems to be doing okay now.

I tell my mom I will see her later and head to Ken's for an early Christmas dinner. When I get to their place, Jeni is playing the Puff Daddy and the Family album. I tell her she never seems to let me down when it comes to music, and she laughs. They're both preparing dinner, so I decide to go out and help their neighbor shovel snow. Her name is Olga, and she is a tall white woman with short white hair. She's also the head surgeon for Cook County Hospital. I always have cool conversations with her about food. Although her vocabulary is far above mine, I use context clues to understand what she is saying. We get along very well. The first few times we spoke, it was basically her telling the boys and me to keep it down when we were too loud in the backyard.

"You have amazing networking abilities," Jeni says. "Our friends like you more than they like us."

I find myself hanging with Ken and his friends Bob

Muzikowski, Marty Murray, and Russ Greenberg a lot. I sit, listen, and learn every time I'm around those guys. Russ manages Ken's real estate business, and he calls the rowing team anytime he needs help with simple labor so we can make extra cash.

As we sit down for dinner, Ken tells me we have a new coach named Marc Mandel.

"That's cool. I hope he can handle everyone."

"He will be great, make it easy for him."

Jeni has set out a beautiful dinner, and we eat until we can't eat anymore. The food is to die for, and afterwards we open gifts. I know I can't give Ken and Jeni something they don't already have, so I wrote them a beautiful card and give them chocolates. Jeni gives me a book to read called The Four Agreements. I open the cover and quickly read over the main points, and I am instantly hooked. I open another gift, and it is a small gold chain that I admired at the mall once when Ken and I went to get clothes for Winnifred. I choke up a bit and tell them I can't thank them enough. I wonder, Who am I that life is so wonderful to me? Life used to be so bad for me that jumping off a bridge was a daydream. People like to say life gets better, but to me it isn't just a saying. It is the truth.

I sit at the table, deep in my thoughts like Kevin from The Wonder Years, not hearing the words that are coming out of Ken and Jeni's mouths. Everything fades away, and I think about how Jeni is just like an apple. If you can get past the tough skin, you will see her sweetness. I see the star she really is and will become. I think about Ken too. From the moment I first met him, Ken has exposed me to higher education, Ivy League colleges, healthy living, traveling, finding my purpose, and understanding the needs of the world. He has never given up on us and has been faithful and positive every step of the way. I am grateful for my internship at the Hilton O'Hare hotel, the rowing team, and the entrepreneurship classes. I have accomplished more in two years than I have in the fourteen years before.

....

I'm back at school after Christmas break, and it's amazing catching up with my teammates. Alvin got a new job working at a shoe store in the North Riverside Mall, and he tells me to come to his job for a hook up on shoes. He also tells me he has a new car, and I can't wait to see it.

A couple of weeks ago, Alvin and I ate at IHOP, and he somehow got the phone number of a Mexican girl named Maria who doesn't speak any English. He is still seeing her, and I ask how they communicate.

"We point."

I laugh, "I don't even want to know what that means."

He tells me he's always wanted a girl that doesn't talk his ear off.

Josh is busy being a teenager, making people laugh. He has dreams of going to Second City and hiring me as his booking agent. Josh brags about not being a video game crack head anymore. He said writing jokes takes up all his time now. Elliot is working part time as a cook at the Marriot Hotel. Pookie G. is talking a lot more and has been spending time at home. He is such a homebody. His mom is dating a guy who looks like he's fresh out of the joint. Every time we go to Pookie G.'s place, the guy is sweeping the floor, and there is never any dirt. He only ever gives us head nods and says, "What up, lil niggas?"

We're all really excited to meet the new coach, so I meet Alvin after class and we walk down to the gym room together. Alvin tells me about his brand new '98 Mercury Mountaineer.

"Dude, how did you afford that?"

"I will tell you after practice."

We walk into the gym room and see the new coach. Marc

Mendel is a skinny guy with pale skin and freckles. He has curly red hair that matches the red rings around his eyes. It looks like he's never slept. He looks innocent, and I feel like he may not last a single day in this school. Ken brings us all in.

"Okay, guys, listen up! Get dressed, and I will introduce you to the new coach and we'll start practice."

In the men's locker room, Josh says, "What the hell? Our new coach is the male Punky Brewster."

"I know, man," I tell him. "I have to talk to Ken about this."

"You better, because I will clown this guy all year."

Alvin tells Josh to calm down, and we get dressed and walk back upstairs.

Ken introduces us to Marc and asks if he'd like to say a few words.

Marc stands up. "Hey, guys, I'm happy to be here and I promise you if you do what I ask, I will make you guys fast."

"We will do everything but wear that damn spandex," Josh tells him, "because we are blessed and can't have people staring."

We start laughing.

"Yeah, man, we can't wear that."

Marc agrees and starts looking at our hands. "You can tell a dedicated rower by their hands. The more calluses you have, the harder you work." Our hands don't look like the other rowers we know, like Coach Jessica.

"Okay, sixty laps around the gym," he says, starting to run. We quietly mumble complaints about having to do sixty laps. Ken runs with us as well, and he, Marc, Pookie G. and I are in front the whole time. The gym isn't that big, so sixty laps is really only two miles, but after thirty laps we are all slowing down.

"I'm sure regular life is harder than this," Marc screams out. "Come on, guys, push it!"

Marc is in top shape, and while we're running he tells us he wouldn't ask us to do something that can't be done, so he will always be right there doing it with us. Marc slows down and gets behind me.

"You're the captain…earn my respect!"

He keeps running a few paces behind me so there is no room for me to slack. I push myself until every last lap is completed. I can't breathe. I squat down, but Marc tells me to stand up, it's good for me. While the other guys are finishing up he asks me to help him set up the erg machines. I'm really dying and showing it.

Marc tells me, "We get tired but don't show it—it's a sign of weakness."

All the other guys finish and start walking towards the door. Marc stops them.

"Hold up, no water right now. We're not finished warming up." Some of the guys begin complaining, but I tell them we're not done yet.

Alvin throws his hands up. "Oookay, let's get it over with." We sit on the rowing machines and Marc walks over and sets the timer for forty minutes.

"Oh, hell naw," Josh yells. There is a mixture of laughing and coughing because we are so tired.

Marc gives us all a smirk. "Oh, hell yes. Okay, let's go, arms only."

We row arms only until they go numb, then add arms and body, and then full body. He critiques every movement we make. I feel like it is my first day rowing, as if I'm not doing anything right. Marc is a technique man, and he stares at every drive I take on the erg, staring at my feet, hands, face, and back. It is hard for me to concentrate. Alvin lets go of the handle.

"This is crazy!"

We've all been waiting for the first person to say it. Marc

tells us all to pause. He steps over to Alvin and passes the handle back to him.

"You never let go of this oar. You just gave up on every person in the boat. You want to do that to yourself, fine, but don't forget you're not in that boat alone. We are all one in that boat."

Alvin grabs the handle with his head down.

"When you are in that boat, people are going to watch you more than they watch themselves. You guys are super strong, and I'm going to give you the tools to win a race. Back to catch and row."

I look at Marc, and I know he is the nightmare that I asked for who will push me past my limits, until I know that I am fully awake and always ready to go.

After practice, Marc talks to us one by one and explains our strengths and weaknesses. He tells me that there is a Chicago indoor racing championship in a few weeks that I will be racing in.

"It's a 2000 meter piece. I am going to test you tomorrow and we will prepare you for it." I nod. "Good job today, Arshay."

I think about what he said. A 2000 meter piece on the erg is painful. I tested myself in the summer, and I rowed 2000 meters in seven minutes and thirty-one seconds. I want to beat that time. When I walk into the locker room, all the guys are complaining again. I tell them what I think, that I think Marc is great, a welcome change.

"I know," Alvin says, "but to start off that way is insane."

The other guys agree.

Pookie G. isn't happy either. "I cox the boat and still have to do it!"

Josh tells me he thinks Marc is a red-headed monster. I agree, but I know he is going to make us faster so I'm willing to wait it out.

We head outside, and I notice everyone from Alvin's neighborhood driving around in nice cars. There are sixteen-year-olds who I know have no license and no money driving around in drop tops.

"Alvin, what's going on and why does everyone have nice cars? Even Pooh Nigga is driving around in a new truck."

"Don't say nothing," Alvin tells me, "but there is this white man, a junkie."

"Dude, that's illegal."

"Yeah, man, of course it's illegal. It's fifty bucks."

I'm in shock because the whole neighborhood has a new car. I tell him I'm going to take the train home, and he tells me he's going to work and then pick up Maria.

"Oh, yeah, I will get over there to get shoes this week."

"Cool, I will give you two pairs for fifteen dollars." I laugh and tell him I will see him at practice tomorrow.

When I get home, my mom is upset, and I know it's because she is having problems with my little brother. There are times I want to seriously knock him out. I try to spend time with him, but I'm not who he looks up to. He admires Shaundell, who has girls, tattoos, friends with sweet cars, and a great social life. Isaac thinks hip hop music videos are the coolest thing he ever saw and feels like Shaundell life looks the same; but they don't show the jail, paranoia, child support payments, funerals, and crying mothers. He has a hard head, so my words don't penetrate. What pisses me off about my brother is that every time he gets upset with my mom he brings up her past. She's learned to deal with that because she is aware that anyone who changes their life might encounter a loved one that drives them back to the thing that almost killed them. Without bringing up Isaac, I tell my mom that I will cook dinner tonight. I know that will make her happy. I head into my room and tell Isaac we can go to the store and get junk food, my treat. He is happy about that.

....

During fourth period, Mr. D. tell us that it's time for the annual Black History project competition. We team up with a partner and select a person, movement, or time from Black History to present to the whole school. All the public schools are involved. If you do well and make it to the top ten in your school, you will go to regionals, and the top ten from there will go to city finals and they will choose a winner. Alvin looks at me and says we're partnering up. I want to partner with someone who will put a lot of focus into this, but I figure I will give it a try with Alvin.

Mr. D. tells us to get into our teams and choose a subject. We both decide on African Americans in sports during the 1960's.

Alvin says, "Let's just do this to get a decent grade, man."

"You know we have to buy a presentation board, do research, and a lot more right?" He tells me he knows, and I tell him I'm going to stay after him to get this done.

"Trust me, I know that too." We both laugh.

After class, I walk Grace to the bus stop quickly because Marc is a no-nonsense coach who doesn't condone tardiness. Grace expresses her gratitude to me because I've stuck by her and always walk her to the bus stop. It sounds like she is ready to give me a shot. I tell her we will talk tomorrow and then run to practice. There are old men who sit on the porch every-day drinking beer that notice me running back to school after walking Grace to the bus stop.

"There he go again."

I change in the locker room and then run up to the gym where Marc and the guys are already running. I join the line and Marc informs us we have to do ten more laps. They all look at me, pissed off, and Alvin shakes his head. I guess, in a way, I'm hard headed. I just don't like giving up on people or things unless they're hurting me. I'm not sure if wanting to be with Grace is hurting me.

After the run, Marc sits us down and explains his goals. He tells us we will spend this winter running, rowing on the erg machine, visiting college campuses, being tutored, and then more running. We laugh.

"You guys are going to Philly again during spring break, and it's going to be a hard training camp. They are building a new rowing site on the South Side, and you guys will help build it.

"This is going to be a great year, and if you guys behave like men I will take you to the famous Buffalo Joe's and visit my college, Northwestern University."

I ask him what Buffalo Joe's is.

"The best wings spot in the world." Josh asks if they have watermelon in a very sarcastic tone, and we start laughing again. Marc doesn't crack a single smile.

We spend the next two weeks running and doing the erg machine non-stop. I am in prime shape and run everywhere. Everyone in school is noticing our transformation. Marc is the right man for the job; he is a lion in sheep's clothing. He looks so innocent, but his roar is strong.

....

On Saturday, Marc picks me up for the Chicago Indoor Rowing competition. My last time for 2000 meters is seven minutes and twenty-nine seconds. I'm hoping to beat it by at least ten seconds. When we arrive, there are hundreds of people in the gymnasium. Once again, I am the only brown face in the crowd. I am set to race in the eighteen-and-under age group. I notice there are college kids that are eighteen-year-olds in my section, so I get a little nervous. Marc tells me that no one here is in my league.

"You're stronger than any kid I've seen on the erg machine.

Remember, you have a right to be here and a right to win. I have high hopes for you, Arshay." That is all I need to hear, and I am ready. The power of speaking the right words to a young person can do something magical. You feel unstoppable.

I see some of the kids from the St. Ignatius race. I look at them, and they glare at me with their infamous smirks. I can't wait to race them again. I know to them we are just the kids who ran into the brick wall.

I sit on the erg machine, and Marc is right there next to me to coach me. He is more intense than I am. I can see the press from Rowing News behind me in the mirror.

"To the catch. Ready. Row!"

I drive back with all the strength I can gather from my legs. The wheeze of the fans from the erg machine fills the room. People are getting busy.

My arms are giving out. Marc has to push me through the last couple minutes, yelling, "It's heart and mental from here. You will be the champion!" I close my eyes and max out when there are 100 meters left.

"Stop!" Marc yells. "Look around you, everyone is still rowing."

I won first place! And I am so tired I can't get off the machine. I win a medal, and the journalist from *Rowing News* tells me they will send me a copy of the newspaper with "Arshay Cooper, First Place" and the names of the guys I competed against. I am happy to have more material for the wall. I have become a fan of the awards that come with a strong work ethic.

Afterwards, I ask Marc to drop me off at Ken's place where I am going to meet Alvin. I can't wait to share the good news.

As we're driving, he says he has to talk with me about something. It sounds serious.

"I have been questioning your leadership because you've been late to all of our practices. It's not fair for the guys to do extra work because you're walking a girl to the bus stop. Meet her after. I'm down for love, but you have a responsibility to your guys. Alvin stepped up to tell me the truth about how much this person means to you."

In my head, I'm thinking that everyone deserves that high school sweetheart, but quickly I realize I'm not anyone's sweetheart. Grace is my friend, but the person that makes me smile is also the same person that makes me frown. I realize Marc is teaching me about discipline, but I have a feeling he knows more and wants me to get over her and stay focused.

"I got a taste of what I can do today," I tell Marc, "and whatever I have to do to see more success, I'm going to do it."

When I get to the house, Alvin is there playing Ken in chess. The game is pretty serious. I know Alvin was on the chess team in junior high school and won a few awards. Ken is extremely focused. I feel like his pride would be hurt if he lost to a high school kid from the West Side, especially Alvin. Alvin has grown on Ken; he used to believe that Alvin didn't deserve to be on the team. Ken is turning red because Alvin is winning, and Alvin is shaking because he knows he is going to win.

"Checkmate!" Alvin is laughing and jumping as if he's won the state championship. Ken is not happy.

"It's just a game," I tell Ken.

"I'm taking you all to play chess next week at the community center." I tell him I don't play chess.

"You all will learn." He congratulates me on my rowing win. I notice that Ken and I are both sore losers.

....

Ken drives us all to the ABC Community Center to learn how to play chess. A lot of his entrepreneurship students are there as well. Ken has asked Lorne, a friend of Jeni's from law school, to come in and teach the class. Lorne is a very odd guy. He is white, with dark, curly hair and a Cosby sweater. He has a very dry sense of humor and tells what Malcolm calls "Seinfeld jokes." When we talk, he just looks at us as if we aren't speaking English. Alvin tells me he doesn't think Lorne is normal, but he's smart as hell.

Alvin and Ken make a bet that if Alvin can beat Lorne in chess, Alvin can use Ken's car for the weekend. If Alvin wins, we plan to cruise all weekend. The new car that Alvin purchased from the drug addict was already stolen. He was held at gunpoint by a guy he knows well from the neighborhood. Alvin told me the guy stole it to do dirt. He told Alvin not to do anything stupid since he only paid fifty bucks for it. He made me promise not to tell anyone else.

When the match starts, we stand behind Alvin while Ken stands next to Lorne. Ken is stressing and tells him not to lose this game.

"My car is on the line, Lorne."

"Chill out, this kid doesn't stand a chance."

"What you say, fool?" Alvin pipes up, "I have home court advantage."

I don't know what's going on, but I know it is close. Alvin is shaking. He always shakes when he is mad or nervous. Lorne doesn't look worried, but Ken does. Before I know it, Lorne wins the game.

"Dude, you didn't stand a chance. Go get some more practice."

Ken cracks a smile for the first time today. Alvin gets up and calls Lorne "garbage" and walks away. Lorne eggs him on, but I try to distract everyone and ask Lorne if he's going to teach us chess or not. Alvin isn't a big fan of Lorne. We play chess the rest of the day.

....

I can't sleep. I have decided to tell Grace that she has to give "us" a shot, or I am going to move on and explore other options. This friend-zone madness has taken its toll on me. I can't sleep because I am starting to come to my senses and realize that if she wanted to be with me, it would have happened already. It's been a while since I asked her about our relationship so I am still holding onto an ounce of faith that she will say we should go for it. I decide to force myself to sleep because this is so confusing and love sucks.

Before practice, I tell Alvin to let Marc know that I will be a few minutes late because I have to talk to Grace.

"Dude, we'll have to run."

"No, he will understand." Alvin wishes me good luck. I walk her to the bus stop, and while she is talking, I rehearse what I am going to say to her. My heart is pounding, and my legs are giving out.

"I think this is probably the last time I will say this, but I like you. What do you want to do about us?" She stops and looks at me. "Girl, I like you a lot."

"I know, and I like you a lot."

"Well, that's progress."

She stops me. "But I can't give you what you deserve."

I feel like a stupid little boy.

"You know I will need some time before I feel comfortable being just your friend," I tell her.

"Yes. And Arshay... I have always been honest with you."

"I know. I just haven't been honest with myself."

I don't know if Marc, Alvin, Josh, or anyone else has ever felt what I am feeling right now. It is the worst feeling, like my chest is being cut open with a knife and a blow torch is blowing away at it. Getting punched in the face would feel better than this, and for the first time ever there is no one around to do it. I tell her I have to go, and she understands. I wave at the old men drinking on the porch. They don't know it is farewell.

I walk into the gym upset, ruined, fully-clothed, and short

of breath. I sit on the erg machine and just go at it. No one
says a word to me or stares. They allow me to deal with what
I'm going through. My thoughts are racing as I am rowing.
She doesn't know that I've trained so hard to transform my
body to look good for her. She doesn't know that I run extra
laps, hurt my teammates, rent love movies, spend hours
daydreaming, draw pictures, skip homework, lose sleep, and
pray for her. She will never know. I tell myself that this is part
of the high school experience. What is high school without a
broken heart? I feel soft, like I'm not being a man; I have never
seen any of my friends like this. I've also never seen them in
love. I repeatedly tell myself that this is not a door closing but
another door opening. I sit on the erg machine torn apart, not
because I let her go, but because it is the right thing to do.

After my workout, Alvin approaches. "I need to holla at
you."

"I know, we have to finish the history project by the end
of the week."

"Yeah, that too, but Preston's boy got into an argument
with SOA, and they're going to stomp this dude tomorrow
after school. Preston will probably try to help."

"Damn, man. Preston can't do that; these guys are nuts.
Can you say anything to squash it?"

"Naw, man, I tried."

"I will call Preston as soon as I get home."

He nods before asking, "You cool?"

"Yeah, man, for sure."

When I call Preston, he tells me that if SOA jumps his boy
he will have to help.

"Preston, there are eighty of them and five of you."

"I don't care, and if you're not going to help me, it's all
good."

I want to scream at him. Preston is so different now. I tell
Preston to tell his boy to be cool, and maybe nothing will

happen. I call Alvin and tell him that I don't care what the beef is, but we have the power to fix it. It's our responsibility.

"I don't ask for much, but I'm asking you to fix it."

"Alright, I get you."

I hang up, knowing he will. He has a lot of influence over those guys. Even though he doesn't roll with them anymore, they won't forget the times he's had their back. I go to bed listening to The Quiet Storm on the radio to make my night a little easier.

....

The school day goes smooth; Alvin fixed the situation between Preston's friend and SOA. I see Grace in the hallway, and we walk right past each other. My body goes numb for a second and then I'm fine. I take a deep breath and remind myself that it's for the best. I walk past Mr. Edwards, and he tells me to pick my head up. I smile back at him.

After rowing practice, we walk to Alvin's place to wait for Ken. I asked Jeni to help us with our history project because we've been getting nowhere. Ken offered to take us to get the stuff we need for it. When he gets to Alvin's place, we are sitting on the porch with a bunch of kids who can't wait to go to high school to join the rowing team. They've heard about what we've done and the places we have gone. Alvin and I jump into Ken's jeep. The door opens, and the rest of the kids start to climb into Ken's jeep too.

"Hey, what are you guys doing?"

"We want to go too."

"Not right now," Ken tells them, but they won't leave.

Alvin and I pull them out of the car and tell them we will take them out later. I can't help but think how awesome it is that they want to come with us. When I get older and kids see my car, I don't want them to see a chef, a cool guy, or a rower. I want them to see me as hope for the community. Hope is a beautiful thing. You can lose your girl, family, friends, and money, but you can never lose your hope. I want to represent that hope.

We pick up what we need and head back to Ken's house. Jeni sits us down to hear the plan for our project. We tell her we want to talk about the African American sports movement in the 60's. She shakes her head.

"It still sounds like a first draft idea. You guys didn't do any research; this is ridiculous. You guys need to do something more powerful."

"I saw the Black Panthers movie," Alvin says. "That was really good."

"Then focus on something they did. You can talk about their breakfast program, the start of the Black Panther Party, or how radical they were."

I tell her I want to talk about their radicalness, so she sets us up with the internet and tells us to spend a couple hours researching.

We spend two hours taking notes. We learn things about the Black Panthers that we never saw in the movie. Fred Hampton, the chairman for the Black Panthers in Chicago, has a special place in my heart. He was an activist that preached about education, serving the community, and police accountability on the West Side. After he was killed by the cops, drugs began flooding the neighborhoods of Chicago. Reading about this movement is really touching to me and Alvin. He thinks that if we were both teens in the 60's, I would be part of MLK's movement and he would be part of the X movement, because of our personalities. I agree, as long as we are both part of a movement.

Jeni comes back to help us dig into more details and challenges us to be more radical with our project. She is annoyed with how slow we type, and tells Ken we need to take extra computer classes outside of school. I can only remember taking one computer class freshmen year. I look up at the clock, and it is almost midnight, but Jeni is determined to help us get it done and to present it the best way possible. I tell Alvin how much I value Jeni and that I would do anything for her. Alvin agrees.

"Yeah man, she is one of a kind." I look at her like a second mother, and I believe my mom and Jeni are the strongest women I know.

When we present our project in the gym the next week, the school staff is shocked that Alvin is so educated on the project. Ken and Jeni show up to support us, and we get praise for our work.

A few weeks later, we find out that we've made it to the regional finals and will be going to Curie Metropolitan High School to present. Alvin tells me he never thought in million years we would be here.

"It's your work, man, enjoy it."

We head to regionals, but I think our work might be a bit too radical as the testimonies about corrupt politicians turn off some of the judges. Alvin thought that might happen. We are happy with what we've done and what we've accomplished. We learned the truth about the Black Panthers Party and are confident that we will carry their legacy with us.

···

Winter is flying by and the team's hours outside of school are totally dedicated to running, the erg machine, learning crew culture, visiting campuses, study sessions, and entrepreneurship classes. There is no time for hanging out at the mall, watching TV, or chasing girls. Well, Alvin always finds time to chase girls even though he is still with Maria, who has finally learned how to put a sentence together in English.

Pookie G. and Alvin attend church with me on Sundays, and Ken and Winnifred pop up every once in a while. Ken even donated some money to Victory Outreach because he loves their mission and he knows that they get results. Josh has become the little brother of the team, finally opening up about being bullied his whole life and how comedy has helped him. He tells us the popular kids clowned him daily because his clothes weren't name-brand. He says that being bullied hurts way more than getting punched in the face. I second that one because being laughed at makes you want to drop out of school, hurt someone, or hurt yourself.

Josh said he listened to tape cassettes by Redd Foxx, Eddie Murphy, and Richard Pryor. Then he went to school and, before someone opened their mouth to talk about him, he would tell a joke. Every day after that, people would ask him to make them laugh. The bullying stopped. We've all gotten close to him since he began to open up, and we always tell him that one day millions of people will laugh at his comedy.

After all of our ups and downs, I finally feel complete as a team. Marc is the best coach that we could ever ask for. When we run, he runs farther. When we do push-ups, he does more. When we have study sessions, he corrects us. When we watch rowing videos, he quizzes us, and when he sees physical results, he puts us on the erg machine and he evaluates us. We called him the Marcanator.

Before I know it, we are heading to Philly again for spring break training camp. Marc decides to invite other students so we can have reserves. I need extra cash for the trip so I call my uncle Terry and ask if I can work as a laborer for his construction company. Terry has been doing well for a year now since he graduated from the Victory Outreach recovery home in California. He was a severe addict, but when he saw my mother change he decided that he needed to go far away and do the same for himself and his kids. When he came back, he started a construction business and hired young guys to keep them off the street.

On Saturday, I take the train to the South Side and meet my uncle at one of the buildings he is working on. He is one of those old-school uncles who asks all his questions at once and answers them at the same time.

"Where you been? At school. Where ya momma? At home. How you losing weight? Not eating."

Before I can say anything, he grabs me. "Come on, boy, let me show you what you doing."

My uncle has me hanging drywall with him. While we are working, the owner of the building walks in and says hello. She is an older lady with gray hair and dark brown skin. She asks my uncle questions about his life and where he grew up. Turns out they both grew up in the same neighborhood, and they start ticking off mutual friends. The woman asks my uncle if he knows the Lattimores and my heart starts pounding.

"Norman or Dennis Lattimore?" I ask her.

"Yes, Norman is my godson."

I feel my heart throb in my chest. "That's my dad."

She gives me a hug and tells me I look just like him. I give her a fake smile, and she says she is going to call him.

"Please, not now."

"Well," she says, "I am going to give you his number."

"You are so nice," I tell her, "but can you just give him mine?"

She gives me long look and agrees to give him my number. She is excited and says she can't wait to call and talk to him.

I continue working as memories of Norman start coming back. When I would get in trouble as a little kid, my mom would beat me and tell me I was a mistake. When she was on drugs, she would make the same claim, and I never understood why.

....

The first time I met Norman I was nine years old. My mom

told me to come to the door because there was someone she wanted me to meet. I walked to the door and saw him and knew it was my dad. He looked at me with a big smile on his face.

"Hey, I am your dad." I looked down at his hand, and it was full of quarters.

"I am coming to get you this weekend and we will hang out."

"Okay," I nodded eagerly.

"Okay, son, I will see you then." I said goodbye, and he started walking down the stairs. I asked my mom if I could ask him for a dollar. She said yes, so I ran after him and asked him for a dollar. He said he didn't have a dollar bill on him, but would bring me one that weekend. I nodded and walked back up the stairs.

That weekend he came to pick me up for a family Halloween party. My mom didn't buy me a costume, so she covered my face with her red lipstick and sent me on my way. I remember being there and feeling left out because everyone had a costume and no one paid me any attention. He left me with his sister and her son that whole weekend and I had a blast. They were fun and glad to have me. When he picked me up, he took me back to his apartment and introduced me to his mom and dad and brother Dennis; they were all hospitable.

After he dropped me off at home, I told my mom that I had a lot of fun and I wanted to go back soon. I called his number every day after that weekend for months. I must have dialed that string of digits over a thousand times. He never answered. That was the last time I saw him. I would daydream in elementary school that he might come pick me up in his red pickup truck with the cab only big enough for me and him. All the kids from class would ask to jump in the back, and I always let them.

I snap out of my thoughts, and my uncle is looking at me.

He knows what I'm going to say.

"What a coward."

My uncle nods. "But you probably wouldn't be the guy you are today." I smile because I am happy with the guy that I am.

When I get home, I tell my mom what happened at work. She sits and says, "Arshay, Norman was a friend and a bad alcoholic. One day, we both got really drunk, and he kept asking to have sex with me because he said he had a crush on me, but I never liked him like that. After a few more drinks, I told him maybe."

"Oh, no. I can't listen to this."

"Arshay, listen. We slept together once, and I had you. I am happy for that, and you are not a mistake. God wants you here." I tell her that if Norman calls I will talk to him, and she is happy.

"Thank God for alcohol," I mumble sarcastically as I close my door.

The phone rings around nine p.m. and I know it is him. I pick up the phone, and he asks for Arshay.

"Speaking."

"It's your dad," he says, sounding so happy that my attitude suddenly changes. We talk about his godmother, and I tell him what I'm up to. We talk about him and his family. He tells me that he got married and moved to Country Club Hills, which is an hour outside the city. Norman asks if I can come to his place for the weekend to hang out. I tell him I can't do a weekend, but I can come for a day. He wants to know why I can't come for a weekend, and a million reasons run through my mind. Instead, I say that we should start off slow and get to know each other. He gets frustrated and tells me to hold on.

A few seconds later, his wife gets on the phone. "Arshay, we love you and want you to come and stay just for the weekend." I tell her it's very nice to meet her, but can I please speak to

Norman. He gets back on the phone, and I tell him again that I would love to come for a day. He tells me he will call me back, and we hang up.

I'm not sure if I handled it well. One part of me says a visit should be on my terms, and the other part is saying that I should just go with the flow. I do want to know a lot of things about my family. I want to know our history, if I will go bald, where I get some of my bad habits. I just don't feel right so I decide to call back, and we decide to meet later in the week on the West Side at his sister's place.

....

I am walking to meet Norman with butterflies in my stomach. I told the guys on the team the story, and they all offered to come with me. I didn't take them up on it, but it felt good to know they have my back. Josh told me to ask for child support money. He is good at cheering me up with jokes.

When I turn the corner on Kedzie and Douglass, I see Norman and his wife on the porch. They both jump up and give me a hug. Looking at him is like looking at me in the future. He has the same rich brown eyes, curly afro, and chestnut-colored skin. He looks me over, takes a deep breath, and says, "Son."

We head into my aunt's apartment, and they show me pictures of my grandparents, cousins, aunts, and uncles. It is surreal. My aunt seems nervous, and I can tell she just wants everything to work out. Norman was very talkative while I was a little bashful. I couldn't read his wife, as she didn't say much. I open up for twenty minutes about rowing, and they are all agog. Shortly after, we say our goodbyes, and I tell him to keep in touch. I feel good about seeing him, and I know it is something I had to do.

The next week we are off to Philly for spring break. There are seven boys and seven girls plus Marc, Coach Jessica, and

Miss Topel, an English teacher from Manley who I think has a crush on Ken. Having Miss Topel as an English teacher is a blast. She is known for making us sing out a word definition to remember it. She says it's because we read a paragraph once and forget it right away, but when we hear a song twice we remember the whole thing. I've seen Miss Topel cry many times and storm out the classroom. I guess when she decided to make a difference in the world by teaching it didn't include breaking up fights, screaming for forty-five minutes, and being called a cunt every week in the manual.

Miss Topel loves what Ken is doing with the rowing team and feels like it sets us apart, so she decides to tag along and chaperone us during spring break. There are two fifteen-passenger vans; the boy's ride with Marc and the girls with Coach Jessica and Miss Topel. Marc will focus on coaching the guys, and Coach Jessica will coach the girls. The girls are Ana, Leslie, Zinanta, Antonia, Delilah, Shaquis, and Entantra. We spend the whole time listening to Josh crack jokes about us and the girls in the other van. He is one of the only guys who can make Marc laugh. We crack on Josh because every time Marc drops him off or picks him up at home, his grandmother smacks him across the head for something he said. Marc is terrified of Josh's grandmother, and we think she's a little nuts, maybe even packing heat. The old lady never stops yelling. Josh always says if it weren't for his crazy grandmother he wouldn't have any comedy material.

We sleep half of the trip, but Josh stays up the whole time. He tells us he doesn't want to miss anything. He is such a good kid. Josh spends all day making people laugh, but I know that when he gets home to the four walls of his room he feels alone, so we make a pact to cover him with brotherly love.

When we finally make it to Philly, Marc pulls into a grocery store to get food before heading to the youth hostel. There is a Latina girl inside the store and Alvin starts singing

"My, My, My" by Johnny Gill to her while walking behind her. She can't stop smiling. She stops and tells him he has a nice voice and asks how old he is. He lies and says eighteen, which is how old she looks.

"I'm in town for a week for a race. You should give me a call."

He gives her Marc's cell number and tells her to call him tonight. You can tell Alvin has made quite an impression on her.

We get to the hostel, and all the girls complain about the healthy food Marc bought. The guys are fine, since healthy eating is a lifestyle to us now. We cheat a couple times a week, but not around Marc. Marc sits us all down to explain the schedule for the week, and his phone starts ringing. He picks up the phone, and we can hear a muffled voice.

"Can I speak to Alvin?" We all start laughing.

"Who this is?"

"I just met Alvin at the supermarket."

"No, you can't talk to him."

Alvin starts pleading with him, but Marc hangs up the phone, his face beet red. He does not play games when it comes to business. The phone rings again and Marc picks it up.

"You can't talk to him," he says and hangs up again.

She keeps calling, so Marc has to turn his phone off.

"Listen up," Marc says, "we are here to work, this is not a vacation."

I can tell he is also frustrated with the girls because they came out with their hair and nails done and new outfits.

"You are going to work your back off. We will wake up at five a.m. to run hills and then row. Then we'll go to the University and sit in on some of the classes, eat lunch, and go back to the boathouse to row. Every day, guys. That's the plan."

The girls look like someone just stole their man. I am fine with it. Five a.m. does seem a little extreme for spring break, but that's crew culture.

We are at the boathouse at 5:40 a.m. The girls stick around to stretch with Coach Jessica and Marc tells us to run fifteen minutes out and fifteen minutes back while he rigs the boat. We run up a hill for about five minutes and then Alvin stops.

"This is insane. It's early and we're on spring break."

Tyromeo, one of the new guys, nods in agreement. "Marc is extreme."

They all sit on a bench and look up at me,

"Arshay, we're training again later today. We are not running ten more minutes up that hill."

"Okay, we can talk."

We relax for twenty minutes and then run back down to the boathouse. Marc puts the regular rotation in a four boat while Tydon and Tyromeo wait to get on the next round. It's our first time on the water with Marc, and he preaches perfection the whole time. We spend a lot of time on one-handed feather drills to perfect our feathering. He also perfects our posture, drive, stroke, and finish. Marc has the eye of the tiger and almost never blinks when we are on the water. When we're rowing with Marc, we aren't four individuals: we're one rower, completely in sync.

"Guys, now you are a crew," Marc says to us at the end of the day.

I think we've done so well because we've spent hours and hours on the erg machine working on our technique. The college teams at UPenn praise us on how strong we are and can't believe we are high school students. They tell us to perfect our technique, and we will be monsters.

The next morning Marc sends us to run hills again. We run for five minutes, lie on the bench for twenty, and then run back down. Josh is cracking up laughing at the girls rowing because they all have life jackets on and their hair done. They are also complaining and refusing to do simple techniques.

"Uh-uh, I'm not doing that."

The boathouse is connected to the Schuylkill River and to the left is a dam. The girls are near the edge of the dam, and at one point I hear Coach Jessica scream at them to row faster. They are so close to it, I get nervous for them.

I think back to our first race and wonder if that's the way people looked at us when we ran into the brick wall.

After a perfect morning on the water and tanning in the sun, we head to the University for class. I choose to sit in on a psychology class. I am with a Penn student, and we talk about college on the way to the lecture hall. The professor talks about dreams and night terrors, and I am fascinated. The class has every race and nationality present. The students have tape recorders, and I can tell they are there to learn. I always thought that if I don't go to culinary school I would go to an all-black college so I can learn things about my culture that I hadn't learned in high school. After being in this class, I decide I want to go to a more diverse college with different ethnicities, religions, and economic backgrounds. My goal is to try to be the best I can be in everything I do. I don't want to be the best only among those who look like me, but also those who don't. I don't think the Cosby Show is just the best black sitcom on TV, I think it is the best sitcom on TV, period. I want to expand my mind and learn about everything and everyone. I also know to study true lost Black History. I will have to learn on my own.

Ken flies out to Philly that night to spend a couple days with us, and Miss Topel can't keep her eyes off him. I tell her he is taken. She laughs and says that she knows and to relax. The coaches are irritated with her because she was caught sneaking junk food to the girls who complained about healthy eating. We are blessed to have a normal teacher here.

....

There are two days left of training before we go home and so far spring break has been all blood, sweat, and tears. We've worked our backs off like Marc said. We run up the hill this morning and lay on the bench as usual, but we are so tired that we fall asleep. I wake up to Alvin.

"Here comes Marc!"

I look up and see him running towards us in his purple Northwestern jacket. I don't know how long we were asleep, but we jump up and start running uphill. Marc is screaming something at us, but we keep running as if nothing happened. Marc is on our tail until we get back to the boathouse. I know we're about to catch hell.

We walk into the locker room, and he throws his clipboard against the locker and yells from the top of his lungs, "Did I catch you guys sleeping? Did you guys do this every day?"

We are all silent.

"Again, did you do this every day?"

Quietly, I say, "Yes."

"I trusted you," he screams. I put my head down. He is so angry.

"I give you guys all I have and you don't give it back in return. You know what they're saying about you? You're a joke, you are just athletic, that you don't belong here. I thought everyone was wrong. You guys almost fooled me."

We don't say a word; we are so disappointed in ourselves. Marc stops screaming and tells us that we have rights, "The right to be here, the right to win, and the right be rowers. You just don't know it." He picks up his clipboard and walks out of the locker room.

"We gonna wear the spandex or what?" Josh jokes, trying to cut the tension.

I jump up and walk into the workout room. I reach into

my gym bag and grab a CD, put it in the boom box, and sit on the erg machine and row. All the guys come in; Alvin sits next to me, the others sit to my right, and we row. Tydon is screaming as he rows. We just let it all out. This machine allows us to let go of our anger, our past, our disappointments, and our sorrows.

Tupac's "Dear Mama" starts playing, and I have a moment. We have a moment. We stop rowing and begin to rap along to the song.

> *"A poor single mother on welfare*
> *Tell me how ya did it*
> *There's no way I can pay you back*
> *but the plan is*
> *to show you that I understand*
> *You are appreciated."*

It means something to all of us. No matter what inner city you are from in America, when it comes on, you stop what you're doing and you rap along with Tupac. It is our story in a song.

Marc walks in and stares at us. He turns the music off.

"Grand Rapids, Michigan."

We look at him, confused.

"There is a big high school race there in the summer; we will prepare for that."

"We won't let you down, coach."

I know that this is the beginning of a new era for us. Nothing has to be said; this is the end of us playing games. We have the eye of the tiger.

PART 8
MICHIGAN

The sun is shining down on us as we recline in the boat, enjoying the breeze. Our new ritual is to lean back and enjoy the water after a hard day of practice. The same water that we used to fear has become our place of refuge. We don't just live to row but row to live. It's been over a month since Philly, and we've been breaking our backs to get ready for the big race in Michigan.

This year has been very good for me. A few weeks ago, I won another indoor rowing competition. This time it was a national race for U.S. Rowing. I am ranked #1 in the city and #35 in the country for Junior Men 2k. I am excited to see if I can Google my name and have my score pop up. I also broke my record, testing at seven minutes and two seconds for seventeen-year-olds. I won a leadership trophy at the Manley Athletic Awards Ceremony. I also won the award for Best Culinary Junior at Manley.

Pookie G., Alvin, Elliot, Josh, Tyromeo, and I have grown stronger as a team. We volunteer together and helped build a new boathouse on the South Side and have become friends with other rowers in the city. Josh entertains everyone during physical labor and spends a lot of time trying to set Marc up with female rowers. The other teams respect us now, and we respect them. Although it's not encouraged to challenge other teams during practice, we secretly have, and we smoke them every time.

Marc finally trusts us and has all the faith in the world in us. Every time we sprint, do push-ups, or wall-sits, I challenge Marc, but to no avail. He is really good. I've become competitive and brutally hard on myself. People always tell me that I'm young and should enjoy being a teenager, but to me it's only temporary fun. Being a teenager is all about fake friends, being broke, and a constant battle for popularity.

While I lean back in the boat, I think about Ken's first speech in the gym when he told us that if we went on this journey with him, we would succeed. I think having a million dollars would be fantastic, and being on TV or the radio would be cool, but giving a kid your word and watching them change must do something on the inside that's better than what those other things can do for you on the outside.

"Hey, guys, look up." Pookie G. interrupts my daydream.

A group of black people on the bridge are giving us fist pumps and yelling, "Go get it." We give them fist pumps back. We figure that they looked down and saw all the white teams, and we're the only black guys so they want to show us some love. We got that all the time at the lagoon.

Pookie G. asks us, "What's the most embarrassing thing that ever happened to you guys?" We start laughing.

"You don't even want to know," Alvin shakes his head.

"Do tell," I say, curious.

"When I was in sixth grade, this boy was talking trash and I knew I could beat him up. I told everyone in school to watch me knock this kid out at lunch. So when I got to lunch, all the girls and boys were waiting for me to do it. I got up and walked towards him while everyone was looking and got close enough to hit him. Before I could, he pulled out a Butterfinger candy bar and whacked me across the forehead, and I passed out."

We start cracking up, and Alvin tells us that when he opened his eyes everyone was laughing, saying he got knocked out by Butterfinger.

"I know that commercial, 'Don't lay a finger on my Butterfinger,'" I tell him, laughing. "What about you, Josh?"

Josh thinks about it for a second. "I was in second grade, I think. Before class started, I was outside, and my friend dared me to go and do the moonwalk in front of the girls. So I go over and do it, and I just kept going. It was easy because it was raining a little, but I slipped in the mud and landed on my face, and everyone started laughing. My older cousin just turned around and acted like he didn't know me."

Everyone makes a face.

"Ooh."

"Ouch."

"Damn."

"That one is rough," I tell him. "What about you, Pookie G.?"

"I can't think of one. You go first and come back to me."

"Okay, mine was in third grade. This kid Rashad had all the cute girls. I mean, they all liked him. I was confused because he had so many scars on his face but it always glowed. So I went to my Cousin Jen Jen's place one day and started a fight with her because I knew she would scratch my face up. She scratched me up pretty bad, and my mom was pissed.

"The next morning I got up for school and put a handful of Vaseline on my scarred face to look like Rashad. I walked into the classroom, and my teacher took one look at me and said, 'Boy, if you don't wash that Vaseline off your face.' All the girls were pointing and laughing. I guess he was just good looking."

All the guys laugh. "Don't worry, that story is going to get you a fine chick one day," Josh assures me.

We start to row back to the dock, still laughing.

....

After practice, I head to Ken and Jeni's place because they've asked if I can babysit Winnifred while they go out. I say yes, but I'm nervous because Winnifred isn't even three years old yet. She jumps into my arms every time she sees me, but she's so little, and it's my first time watching her. When I get there, Winnifred is in her room. I open the door, and she is staring in the mirror with her right hand up in the air.

"Don't raise your hand while I raise mine," she says to herself and drops her arm. She points at the mirror. "And don't talk while I talk."

I shake my head; she is intense for a three-year-old. I close the door and think that she'll either be a good actress or completely nuts.

When Ken and Jeni leave, I search through the VHS box to find a kids movie for Winnifred. I see American Beauty written on a tape and pop it in. The TV is in the kitchen, across from the table, so I get up and call Leona's to order a pizza. I hear a shower running on the TV and a deep voice speaking, and look over to see Winnifred looking at it strangely. I walk over to the TV and see Kevin Spacy "being a man" in the shower. I shut the TV off fast. Apparently, American Beauty is not the same as Sleeping Beauty. One disaster down.

I finally find a kids movie for Winnifred. We watch while we eat pizza.

I always look forward to chilling at their place. This big house speaks to me, and I feel at home here. I hope that one day I will have something just like it. I like using the house, and other things, as my motivation. Sometimes I hang around after practice to watch the college rowers practice and then get into fancy cars afterward. I love to tag along with my mom to hear inspiring speakers. Sometimes I stop what I'm doing to watch the executive chef create art at the Hilton. My favorite thing is to sit in on meetings with Ken and his investors, just listening, although a majority of time I don't understand a single word coming out of their mouths.

I think that taking note as I surround myself with excellence makes it easier to win in life. It's like being on a basketball team with Michael Jordan, Scottie Pippen, Magic Johnson, and Larry Bird. If I lose, it's my own fault.

I once told Alvin, "If a kid walks into a church and says he wants to usher, the church won't say no. If a teenager walks into a community center and says he wants to help with the kids even if there isn't a budget to pay, they won't say no. If a boy walks into barbershop and asks to clean and sweep hair so he can learn how to cut hair in return, they won't say no. If I walk into the best restaurant in this neighborhood and ask to help out for free so I can learn, they won't say no."

Young people have the time, but they don't want to put in the work to get what they want.

When Ken and Jeni get home, Winnifred and I are watching School House Rock. I can tell they've been fighting. When they fight, I usually tell them disturbing news from the neighborhood, which brings them back down to earth. They forget their fight and engage because they genuinely care about the surrounding communities. I am proud of the two of them. Jeni is about to graduate law school and become a public defender, and Ken is receiving awards and press for his good deeds in Chicago.

We are two weeks away from the biggest race of our lives in Grand Rapids, Michigan. We've been fighting hard all year, and I think we might actually have a chance to win. I haven't seen anyone that can move the boat the way we do at our practice site. We've finally earned the one thing that we were searching for: respect. Respect from our coaches, family, friends, the school, and the football team. It was lonely for us without that respect in the early days of rowing. Marc has worked hard to teach us to respect ourselves, our bodies, our time, our boat, our competitors, our teammates, and the crew culture. When we finally figured that out, the world overflowed with an abundance of respect right into our laps. Manley Crew is ready to make a big impact.

I'm walking down the hallway at school when Mrs. Dunn, the business school teacher, asks me if I'm interested in becoming the class treasurer.

'Sure, no problem."

"Amazing! Come tomorrow after school for our first meeting."

I tell her I'll be there, and a guy from my history class walks up to me.

"Hey, your boy got kicked out of school for good."

"Who?"

"Alvin."

"Dude, stop playing, that's not even funny."

The guy tells me that Alvin set the metal detectors off. Apparently, security rushed him to the side to search him. Alvin told them if they were going to search him, they had to search everybody. The security guard pushed him up against the wall for opening his mouth, and Alvin pushed him back. He says Muhammad slid all the way across the floor.

"That big guy slid all the way across the floor? Yeah, right," I tell him.

"He did. And then he got up and told Alvin he's outta here."

I run downstairs to confront the security guard. Before I can even open my mouth, the guard says, "He's done."

"You guys, man."

"Keep it up."

I start to walk away before I end up like Alvin, but I tell him, "It seems like you were in a violent mood before Alvin even walked through those doors."

I am pissed because I'm not sure if he can row for Manley now that he will be sent to an alternative school. I can't wrap my head around the idea that the school hires these security guards because they are physically imposing. Why not hire strong life coaches, mentors, and preachers in this position for extra work?

I can't concentrate the whole day because of this Alvin situation. After school, I tell the guys what happened and we decide to walk to his house before taking the train to the boathouse. Josh tells us that if Alvin can't row, he's not rowing.

"Don't worry, he will row," I tell Josh, but inside I'm scared and don't know what to do or say.

When we get to his house, Alvin opens the door.

"Dude, I could smash Muhammad right now. Where's Marc?"

"He doesn't know," I tell him.

"Man, people see the guy you used to be and just hold you there."

We let that hang in the air, not knowing what to say.

I speak up, "Whenever we are on the road to success, there is always something that's trying to take us off course. The odds are always against us—never with us—but that's going to make us stronger than the rest."

"Because we're constantly fighting," Josh shakes his head.

"The school doesn't communicate with Marc and Ken. So we won't tell them that Alvin is kicked out. We just show up at the boathouse every day. They don't need to pick us up from school."

The other guys all nod their head. Alvin jumps up.

"Let's train!"

We are pumped up and on our way to row away our aggression. We walk down Kedzie to the Blue Line train, take it to Clark and Lake Street, and then transfer to the Orange Line. When the doors open, we step in and see a middle-aged Mexican couple sitting on the train with a guy standing over them, arguing. The man standing is black, around twenty-five years old, and wearing a gray sweater and jeans that are hang-

ing off his butt. The two men are arguing louder and louder.
The black guy lifts his shirt.

"Nothing scares me; I been shot five times."

He starts pointing at every gunshot wound as he gets more
aggressive. Josh jumps up and walks towards them.

"What is this fool doing?" Pookie G. whispers.

"Hey, where you get shot at?"

The guy looks over at Josh like he wants to destroy him.
"What?"

Alvin mumbles under his breath that now we're all going
to have to jump this guy.

"I asked where you were shot."

"Calumet City."

'You know Lil Larry?"

"Lil Larry from out South?" the guy asks, interested.

"Yeah, I think you know my big brother too," Josh says,
turning to walk back towards the rest of us.

"Oh, snap, what's his name?" the guy asks, following Josh.

Josh looks straight at us, with his eyes popped wide open,
like, What the hell do I do now? The guy sits down next to us,
and Josh starts throwing out all these names that only black
people have, asking this guy if he knows them. I look at Josh
like he's a genius, and before you know it we are talking to the
guy about Michael Jordan's retirement.

The train stops at the next station, and the guy screams after
the Mexican couple as they depart. Josh has totally succeeded
in distracting the guy from doing something he might regret.
When we get off the train at Ashland, Alvin tells Josh that he's
stupid but brave.

Josh throws his hands in the air and yells, "Game chang-
ers," and laughs.

....

We have a blast on the water. Marc is on the motor boat with his bullhorn. He tells us we're rowing like champs today,

"You guys have earned it. We're going to Northwestern and Buffalo Joe's this weekend." We get super excited and lie back in the boat listening to the sound of the water. Alvin tells Pookie G. he may win coxswain of the year for calling us every name in the book.

"The angry coxswain," I tell him.

"Whatever it takes to get the job done," Pookie G. says with a smile.

After school, I head down to Mrs. Dunn's room for our class meeting. When I walk into the classroom, everyone is sitting at a round table. There is one seat left open, and it is right across from Grace. I sit, on guard. At the table are Derrick, Grace, Sherry, and Carla. Grace is the vice president. I haven't talked to Grace in months, and it feels strange to be sitting here not looking at her. I keep my face fixed on Mrs. Dunn. I can feel her energy trying to get me to acknowledge her, but I'm sure she feels my energy dying to leave the room. I am definitely strong enough to sit in the same room as her, I just don't want to.

Mrs. Dunn talks about the roles and responsibilities that we have in the positions we hold, but all I can think about is the upcoming race. I've learned to block things out of my head and guard my heart at the same as I guard my teammates. I haven't talked to my dad since seeing him, and it hurts a lot less than last time. I've learned to count my blessings, and there are always more positives than negatives. I've learned how to strengthen myself.

"Arshay, what do you think?" I look up and realize she's asking me a question, and I have no idea what she is talking about.

"Um…I have a tight schedule, but wherever there is a need I'm happy to help," I tell her, hoping it has anything to do with her question.

"Awesome."

The meeting goes on for ten more minutes, and then we're dismissed. I pack up slowly so I don't have to walk out with Grace, but I notice she is moving slow too. I speed up and rush to the door, and somehow she is right there. I drop my pride and return her look.

"Hey you," I say, smiling. I feel her happiness.

"I've missed you, Arshay."

"Sorry for being distant."

"It's okay, you're right here."

She smells like maple, and I start to get flooded with memories. I feel dizzy. Her words are smooth and she is so beautiful. I know she wants to share her frustrations and everything she's going through, but she doesn't. Derrick walks out of the classroom and passes us, and she quietly loses herself for that second. I see it in her eyes.

It hurts, but I let go of the possibility of "someday" because no one gets out the friend zone unless all other options are completely gone.

"Okay then, my friend, I have practice, but we are going to hang Big Head."

"Really? That's perfect."

"See you tomorrow."

We both walk off in the same direction without saying a word; I head downstairs and she heads upstairs. I feel mostly fine. Some people say the heart does what it wants and you can't control it. I think it's what you feed the heart. For the first time, I was able to stand next to her and not be totally awestruck. I decide I will keep that poem until the last day of school.

Saturday morning is beautiful as we head to Northwestern University in Evanston. Alvin, Josh, Pookie G., Elliot and I are pumped. It is just a short ride from the city. Once we start seeing people wearing purple everywhere, we know we are there. The buildings are imposing gray monoliths and the campus is spotless, situated on beautiful Lake Michigan with private student access to the beach.

"This is a good school to come to for rowing," Marc tells us, "and all you guys should think about filling out an application."

"Maybe I will," Josh says, looking around.

We head to the athletic facility and can tell that the guys there are serious about working out. Everyone is in amazing shape. We see where Marc gets his work ethic from. We stay in the athletic facility for an hour and watch the guys train, stealing workout methods from the strength and conditioning coach in the cardio room. Marc walks us around the entire campus and gives us the history of each building. We are constantly learning. We lie out on the grass and crack jokes on each other. Seems like college life is everything A Different World cracked it up to be. We walk over to Buffalo Joe's, and I tell Marc these better be the best wings we've ever had.

"Get the jalapeño wings. They're the best if you like spicy."

We take his advice and tears are flowing from how spicy they are. He wins. I have never tasted a better wing.

"Yeah, Arshay," Josh says, "that's because the only wings you've had is Harold's, Leon's, or Uncle Remus's."

"Exactly," I tell him.

This is our first cheat meal with Marc and everyone is so relaxed. He is a perfectionist, and he's taught us to aim for precision in everything we do; we've taught him to relax and live a little. We love Marc and he loves us, and the family continues to grow. Ken and Victory Outreach have taught me to have vision and to see where I want to be and what to do to get there. I feel like even if we stop now, we've accomplished what Ken wanted from us. We succeeded the moment we stepped in the boat for the first time. As the captain, my vision is for the guys to know that we're not just a team, we're a movement. As the first black men in this position, we can make history and be heroes. I don't want people to look at us and see students, or rowers, or our skin color. I want them to see Hope.

To our parents, we may be a rowing team. To our competition, we may be a joke. But in reality, we are a force. Our school is our base, and we need to protect it like soldiers. If there is a fight, we should break it up, no questions asked. If there is a fire drill, we should help, no questions asked. If our coaches ask us to run a mile, we should run two, no questions asked. The person to our left or our right is not just a teammate, he's a brother.

A captain is not chosen just for ability, or talent, or strength, but for their leadership. Captains should be the first to step foot in the boathouse and the last to leave, not the coaches. A captain understands that every push-up, sit-up, diet, sprain, scar, lecture, and sprint is not a punishment but a way of life and a state of mind.

I look around at my teammates: some of their mothers are drug addicts, their fathers are nowhere to be found, brothers are in gangs, sisters are having babies, uncles are in jail, friends are dying, and refrigerators are empty. But we are a beacon of light. We aren't making the same impact that the Tuskegee Airmen did, or winning like the University of Texas at El Paso basketball team has, or going to the Olympics like the Jamaican bobsled team, but we are making a big difference to our families and those who come in contact with us. We mean the world to them. We went into this thinking we would change the sport of rowing like Jackie Robinson did baseball, but the sport of crew has changed us. We are becoming Dr. King's vision of a beloved community.

....

The music is banging, the room is dark, and some of the best skaters in Chicago are out to skate. We are at Rainbo Roller Rink on Clark Street. Manley always treats the students to an outing towards the end of school year. Rainbo scares me at times because I've heard stories of people getting robbed, stabbed, or shot after skate nights. There are over three hundred students present, and we are ending a good year. I give credit to Umoja and small school directors for that.

I don't skate much. I want to lay low because its race week and I'm not much of a skater. I'm sitting at a table in the dining area when someone creeps up behind me and puts me in a chokehold. I tap out right away because I know its Preston. I know his chokehold.

"Sup, Sweet Pea?" He hates that name. It was given to him by Tara, the girl he chased for years and is still chasing.

"What? I tell you about calling me that," he says, trying to put me back into a chokehold.

"Don't shoot."

He laughs and gives me a bro hug. I don't see Preston as much anymore because one month he will be at school and the next month he doesn't show up.

"Coop, I just want to say I'm proud of you, my dude. I should have stuck with crew, but I got caught up in other interests."

"Remember when we were in, like, sixth grade, and the older guys would drive past and you wanted to pretend play it was our car?"

"Yeah," Preston laughs, "that was fun."

"Then we started seeing those same guys from the hood rocking diamond earrings, so we would say, 'Those are my earrings.'" He laughs as we reminisce.

"So we waited until night time to find a firefly and then took the bulbs out and put 'em in our ear to pretend our diamonds were better."

"Yeah, that was like the best three seconds ever."

"I valued those cars and diamonds. I saw the way life has ended up for those guys, and my values changed."

"That's why I said I'm proud of you, my dude." He looks at the carpet, unsure of how to continue. "I'm not gonna lie. I sell drugs, and some of my people is out there so bad, Coop. On the stuff."

"Preston…I'm so sorry. Let me let me know what I can do. There is Victory Outreach."

"I know," he said, getting up. "I'm about to grab some skates."

"Sweet Pea," I say, and he turns back around. "There is always a seat for you on that boat."

"I'll be back, Coop." I withdraw from the fun around me, deep in my thoughts for the next hour.

When I get home, my mom is reading. She's always reading. Sometimes I think she might be too extreme. She nearly passed out a few months ago because she fasted for six days, drinking only water. I have seen the results of her dedication because Shaundell has also entered into the Victory Outreach Home in Rockford. My younger brother Isaac, on the other hand, is a different story. My mom sent him to the home on the weekends to learn some discipline, and he hit the director in the back of the head with a brush, so they sent him back. Isaac is my responsibility, my little brother, so I try to help him.

My mom tells me, "You fight for your kids, and you forgive them, and you pray. Then you wake up the next morning, and you fight for them again, be an example, forgive them again and you pray."

All I know is that we are not where we use to be. We have dinner together, there are no zombies in our hallway, and we have reasons to smile when we wake up and go to sleep. If my family can change, then Preston, Alvin, Josh, and my other friends' families can change, too. I decide to drop my pride and call Malcolm after talking to Preston tonight. I ask how he is doing.

"Honestly, Arshay, I am jealous of you all. My dad hates Jews, man, and he hates Ken. He don't like the fact that a white man is coming and trying to change black kids' lives. So my dad said if I'm around Ken again, he will punish me.

"Did Ken tell you that people are saying he has you guys rowing out there like a bunch of kids rowing a slave ship?"

I'm speechless. I say I am sorry and will try to figure things out. Malcolm asks that I say nothing and just enjoy the ride. I feel bad losing one of the smartest guys I know. I feel like I can't do this anymore. How can a teenage boy go through so much in four years of high school? I knew Ken was being criticized for trying to turn us white, but he was teaching us that we can do and have anything we want regardless of skin color.

On one episode of A Different World, Dwayne Wayne tells a story about fleas living in a jar, constantly jumping and banging their heads on the lid. One day, the lid is removed, and the fleas refuse to jump out into the unknown, essentially putting the lid on themselves. I feel like in my community, people put limits on themselves and their neighbors. I refuse to live that way. I want to be open to any good idea from anyone with heart. I know people are going to judge us, but like my friend Jerome always says, "The only thing worse than people talking about you is when no one is talking about you."

· ·

The team heads to dinner at Ken's place in the middle of the week, and the guys are all hating on me because I keys to his place.

"This comes with a cost. Ken will put me to work," I tell them.

Alvin's and Ken's places have become my second home. My mom works and goes to church a lot, so I usually stay out until she comes home. My siblings are at my grandmother's.

When we walk into the kitchen, Ken and Jeni tell us that Ken was pulled over last night.

"What did you do?" I ask.

I realize that normally, when black people get pulled over, we ask where it happened.

"I dropped the kids off from entrepreneurship class, and they thought I was there for prostitution."

"Wow, that's messed up."

We sit down to eat and talk about the upcoming race and debrief the last couple of weeks. Ken goes upstairs to put Winnifred to sleep, and I follow him to talk. I tell him that last week I went with Victory Outreach to the juvenile center, and it was a really rough visit.

"How so?"

"Well, they asked me to come in and tell my story about my family, brothers, and rowing experiences. As the guys are walking into the seating area, I see them being treated like animals. They had black eyes and busted lips. I know that they are in for something they did wrong, but will they leave any different?"

"That's why you guys are there."

"Yeah," I say, nodding, "we spoke for an hour, but they still had another twenty-three hours in that place."

Ken asks me how I thought I did, and I tell him I remember being terrified, but they listened. When I was leaving the room, a kid I went to elementary school with yelled out my name, and I turned around.

"He gave me a thumbs up. The guards told him to shut up and my heart bled."

"Well, what are you thinking?"

I tell Ken that Lila Leff and Chef Singleton might be mad at me, but I want to skip a year of college and work on the program we talked about.

"City Year?"

"Yes. I want to dedicate one year of my life to full-time service in the Chicago community."

City Year is an education-focused nonprofit; Ken sits on the Board. It pairs seventeen- to twenty-four-year-old mentors with students to support them by focusing on attendance, behavior, and course performance through tutoring, mentoring, and after school programs that help keep kids in school. The organization focuses on the values of leadership, diversity, and community service. I know I would be perfect for City Year and want to help kids avoid ending up in the juvenile system. I tell Ken I will go the cooking school afterward, but for now, reaching out to "little Arshays" is what I want to do. He tells me it's my life, and I need to do what feels right.

"I will set you up to meet them and see if you like it."

I was always told not to do things tomorrow that I can do today. I know before I go to cooking school and get a job, I want to serve. When you look up City Year Chicago, you see a slogan that says, Everybody can be great because anybody can serve. I know I want to be great.

I thank Ken for being a tremendous mentor and allowing me to see what he sees. He is one of many men I look up too that are happy and have friends that adore him. I always know he is going to be fine. Jeni is like a mom that I protect like my own. When I make a call, she is there in minutes. I don't see her hanging out with many people. I think she likes it that way. She kind of reminds me of me sometimes, so I always feel the responsibility to look after her and be an extra eye for Ken. They have been so selfless. I know whatever I choose to do when I get older, I will always make time for their kids and others.

Welcome to Michigan!

I see that sign and nerves instantly shoot down my body. It's the biggest race we've ever been in. I feel like it's our make-or-break moment. We are focused, nervous, strong, lean, prepared, and confident. I can tell we have been brainwashed by rowing because we went from talking dirty on road trips to talking about split times, oar blades, and what boathouse has nice decks. After thinking about the stuff we used to think and say, I believe a brainwashing was necessary.

We park in front of a huge gymnasium and hop out of the van to stretch. High school rowers are everywhere. They all have sleeping bags in their hands because all two hundred students are camping out in the gym overnight. Josh gets out of the van and whistles at all the white girls.

"The land of milk and honey."

"Is that yours or Pryor's?" I ask him, laughing.

"Mine."

We walk into the gym, and it's filled with laughter and people having a good time. Josh insists that even I could have fun here. He stays on my case about relaxing and having fun, and even calls me "Mini-Marc." I do have fun at times, but I've also never gotten over running into a brick wall, and the look on everyone's face when we did.

We sit in a circle, and Marc gives us our shorts. They are little cotton throwback shorts, Manley written in red on the bottom. I am happy with them. Josh makes a comment about the shorts being Daisy Dukes and we laugh, but I look at them and feel proud to be a Manley Wildcat. I feel like we could have been amazing if we'd had the school supporting us the whole time, but it's fine. We are right where we need to be.

We people watch for an hour or so and then Marc tells us to hit the showers. When we walk into the shower room, its community-style and everyone is naked. We agree that is not happening for us, so we shower in our shorts and then head to bed.

At five a.m., Marc wakes us up. I look around, and everybody is still sleeping. He tells us it's time to run, so the five of us start running and sprinting outside.

Afterwards, he says, "While everyone is sleeping, you're working. You guys are the most creative, talented, strongest, funniest guys I know. Words can't express how proud I am of you."

A few hours later, we're at the regatta watching early races. As always, we're the only black people there and we have mixed emotions about it. Some of the guys are focused and don't get bothered anymore; the others say it still bothers them because there should be more of us here racing. A tall man with caramel skin and a long wavy ponytail approaches. He looks Indian or mixed. He shakes Marc's hand and stares at us.

"I consider this a pleasure to meet you all. My name is Coach Tim Fields. I'm coaching one of the races here."

We say hello but he keeps staring at us, intrigued. He pulls Marc aside to ask how he can get involved.

"That's weird," Alvin whispers.

"Yeah, that's how I looked when I got new G.I. Joes."

Marc tells us it's time to race and my stomach drops. We head over to get our boat, and Pookie G. walks us out to the water, loud and clear for everyone to hear. People stare, as usual. We walk out like a drill team, focusing and walking in sync. We don't look anywhere but forward. We are all chiseled, dark, and handsome. Our strong presence tells everyone we are here to win. I know, without a shadow of a doubt, it is our time. We've given up everything this year for today. It is our moment.

Pookie G. yells "way enough" right before we get to the dock, so we wait to get on the water. We drop our hands with the boat resting on our shoulders. It hurts like hell but looks incredible.

I don't care if you're an Olympian, Harvard rower, or test at four minutes in a 2000-meter piece—there are no rowers I would rather row with than these guys. None of us had ever said as much as hello to each other in the halls before rowing, but now we are brothers. Basketball, football, and baseball couldn't have done what rowing has done to this group. It has taken non-athletic, nerdy, small, broken, and uncool kids and made them a family. Every time we get into the water, we are adding something to it that rowing has never seen before.

Each one of us adds our different flavor: Alvin, the gangsta with the big heart; Josh, the funny man with a famous stare-down that distracts all the other rowers. Elliot is the guy with the slick box haircut who pushes one sleeve up and one down on his shirt. And, of course, our coxswain Pookie G., singing and rapping and calling us every curse word in the Book of Ebonics.

We may be a little rough around the edges, but we make the river a little sweeter every time we step into our boat.

We are Suga Water.

···

Josh tells us that after this win we are going to run in the hood with this boat on our shoulders to make a statement. All the boats are lined up, and I count six in total. It is a 1500-meter race. As we slide up to the catch, I close my eyes and wait to hear his voice.

"Row!"

We drop our blades into the water and take off so fast the boat hops on the water. After every stroke, Pookie G. howls. We are pushing hard, and for the first time we are in the lead. Screams and chants are coming at us from every direction. Sweaty palms, hot sun, painful strokes—it doesn't matter. We row with everything we have.

There is a boat on our left that is close, just behind us.

"Okay, Wildcats, power ten in two!" Pookie G. yells, "One. Two. Now get it!"

We begin to smash. We are a half boat past the boat next to us, then a whole boat past. We are in first and gaining speed. There are three boats already out of sight completely. I look to my left, and Marc is screaming and running towards the finish line, pumping his fist. I have never seen him so happy. I look to the right, and I see 500 meters left. I take a look at the other boats and lose focus for just a heartbeat. My oar drops in the water a half-second too late, and it swings towards me as I lose control. The oar flies up and slaps me right below my neck. I fall backwards, and the oar sails behind me. Marc stops and screams. He instantly turns bright red.

I catch a crab. Alvin yells, "Stop rowing! Arshay, get your oar."

Pookie G. screams, "Keep rowing! Arshay, get your oar," as he paddles the water with his hands.

The boat to our left passes us, and another one is quickly approaching. I grab the oar and pull it in front of me and start trying to row. It is hard to get back in sync. The second boat passes us. Pookie G. is yelling, but I hear nothing. I just row as hard as I can. We catch up to the second boat, but I see we are too late—they cross the finish line ahead of us. We finish third.

I drop my body forward onto my lap and cry. I haven't cried in years. When sweat meets tears, it's been a fight. I know I will be reading this in an article. Alvin leans forward and puts his hand on my shoulder. I can't get Marc's face out of my head. I try so hard with everything I have to be perfect, too hard. I am the leader, and I've let everyone down. I failed. I took my eyes off what was ahead of me to see what was behind me, and I am paying for it. Not just me, but my entire team. My actions caused others to fail.

In this moment, with my face in my lap and my heart in

my stomach, I can hear my teammates saying thank you. I look up, and the teams that have passed the finish line are giving us head nods and thumbs up. They are all showing us the utmost respect. There is still one team that hasn't made it past the finish line yet, so we wait and clap for them when they do. While I'm sitting on the boat, I look over at Marc's face. He doesn't show any signs of disappointment, but I know he is. Any coach would be. The only thing I do see on his face is pride. He's never seen anything like this in all his years of rowing. We're a group of black kids from the turbulent West Side of Chicago, surrounded by a group of Midwestern white kids all sharing praise and respect in the middle of a lake. We are all honored to be a part of this, and rowing has helped us achieve Ken's vision for our lives. He once said win or lose, rowing is the tool you use to fix things. Now I understand that. When I was angry, the erg helped, when I needed peace, the water helped, when I needed discipline, the sport helped. Although I feel bad and unworthy of anything right now, I can't help but think a couple years ago some of us were basically the rejects and outcasts of our communities, but now we are considered the solution. We know who we are.

Ken never promised us we would win, but he did promise that we would learn. To me, that's sports.

EPILOGUE

That was the last time we rowed together as a team. We remained best friends, but we had big dreams we wanted to accomplish individually. Marc moved east to become a college rowing coach, and Tim Fields—who we met in Michigan—took over the program. He turned it into the Chicago Youth Rowing Club, focusing on diversity. Some of us helped coach.

Josh was shot and killed a few years later. People say it was a case of being at the wrong place at the wrong time. Friends mourned him and said it was the saddest funeral they'd ever attended. Josh was our medicine; he made us all feel better. He knew exactly what to do and say to fix a situation better than any of us could. I will always love him for that. He taught us that anything and everything can be fixed with laughter. He was so young. I will never understand how a man can kill another man, and then wake up the next morning and go about his day.

I questioned myself, wondering what would've happened if I didn't follow personal dreams. If I forced us to row in college together, would he still be alive? He was supposed to be the next Chris Rock, but my city is violent. I love my city; it made me who I am. But I cannot accept the violence. What if the local police officers, gang members, aldermen, clergy, firemen, doctors, school principals, basketball teams, grocery store owners, prosecutors, and community all got together weekly to BBQ, play games, watch sports on an outside projector, play cards, attend Sunday services, teach their trades, build a park, speak, shake hands, learn names, mentor, educate, swap books, give jobs, and trust like our rowing team did. What would the community look like?

When you walk into the doors of City Year, they tell you a story by Loren C. Eiseley. When Ken questions if he really made a difference in our lives, I remind him of the story.

Once, there was a boy walking along a beach. There had just been a storm, and starfish had been scattered along the sands. The boy knew the fish would die, so he began to fling the fish to the sea. But every time he threw a starfish, another would wash ashore. An old man happened along and saw what the child was doing. He called out, "Boy, what are you doing?" "Saving the starfish!" replied the boy. "But your attempts are useless, child! Every time you save one, another one returns, often the same one! You can't save them all, so why bother trying? Why does it matter anyway?" called the old man. The boy thought about this for a while, a starfish in his hand; he answered, "Well, it matters to this one." And then he flung the starfish into the welcoming sea.

I can never thank Ken enough for throwing me into the water because the sport of crew changed my life.

···

I have been out of high school for twelve years, and I am back visiting Chicago to help my best friend Alvin bury his dad. I live in New York City now, where Ken and Jeni live as well with Winnifred, who was recently the main subject of a documentary titled "Sexy Baby". I'm heading downtown to meet my mom for dinner on State Street, and I pass a Corner Bakery on the corner of Wabash and Monroe. I see a guy inside that gave me some of the worst memories of my childhood.

Preston's sister had a male best friend by the name of Big E. At that time, I was about thirteen years old, and Big E. was about seventeen or eighteen. He was tall and built like a linebacker, with caramel skin, a box haircut, and a personality that lit up the neighborhood whenever he was around. His clothes were always name brand from head to toe, and he had a strong voice. When he spoke, people would just shut up and listen. He had perfect posture, his jeans had the sharpest creases, he was funny, and life for him seemed awesome.

At some point, Big E. developed a strong passion for making my life a living hell. When I was at Preston's place with all of my buddies and the girls from the neighborhood hanging out, Big E. would always show up there looking for Preston sister. Whenever Big E. saw me, he would gather the crowd together.

"Everyone look at Arshay, he had these clothes on yesterday." Then he would lift my arm. "Everyone smell this. His damn crackhead mom can't even afford him deodorant." He pointed out every stain I had. He would check the tags on my clothes and make fun of them for not being name brand. Then he would look me in my eyes.

"Why do you even exist? Why is your mom a junkie? Dude, go home and clean, you should be ashamed of yourself."

Even when I was clean, he would do it anyway, and people would always laugh. He did this every time he saw me, and friends told me he would clown me even when I wasn't around. Big E. crushed me, belittled me, and damaged my spirit. He wouldn't even stop when tears of hatred would well up in my eyes. The guys told Preston to stop inviting me over because Big E. may just show up. I would even call Preston and ask if Big E. would be there before I stopped over,because I couldn't take the heartache. Eventually people stopped laughing along with Big E., but he never quit.

I asked myself what I did so wrong for him to treat me like that. Did I really look that bad? Did I smell? Did I deserve it? If any girls liked me, they wouldn't anymore after Big E. finished talking about me. He gave me a bad reputation in the neighborhood. It made me bitter towards my mom, and it made me question my existence. This guy gave me nightmares. This happened all the time until I moved away.

I had erased Big E. from my memory, and now here he is at Corner Bakery, mopping the floor, sweating, bloodshot eyes, sagging pants, overweight, looking like life has beat him down.

I want to rush into Corner Bakery and say, "It's me, Arshay, remember me? Of course you do. I just want to let you know that I graduated high school and went to the best Culinary Institute in Chicago. I've traveled out of the country numerous times, I've taken vacations on private islands, and have visited forty-six states in this country. I've performed musical poetry in front of Bill Clinton, and he asked to meet me. Yeah, me. He shook my hand and looked me in the eyes and said, 'keep doing great.' I've spoken to and inspired hundreds of kids in different cities. I worked as a private chef with famous people that we grew up watching on television—they've become my friends.

"I have organized Stop the Violence rallies, completed thousands of hours of community service in this great city, and helped create new programs. I have been a leader among leaders. I visit strangers in prisons to inspire them, I've won martial arts tournaments, and I have been a motivator to UFC fighters. I've been on television cooking shows. I was the captain of the first all-black rowing team. I moved to New York, the most competitive city in the world. I've made a difference.

"Also, remember that crackhead mother of mine that you loved to make fun of? She is different; she's been places and seen things she had never imagined. She has helped change lives that seemed unchangeable. She has been clean for seventeen years. She proved statistics wrong. The funny thing is, if she saw you right now, she would love you right here where you stand and she doesn't even know you."

I want to tell him he almost destroyed me. I want him to feel everything I felt back then. I want to walk in and humble him…but life already has.

In crew, you row forward by looking in the opposite direction. I have learned that it is okay to look behind, as long as I keep moving forward.

My fight with the past is over.

The Beginning

ACKNOWLEDGMENTS

I would like to like to express my gratitude to the many people who saw me through this book. To all of those who provided support, kept pushing me, and believed in my story telling.

I want to thank Writers Digest, for without their conference, I will still be sending out query letters. I am deeply grateful for Dara Beevas, Patrick Maloney, and the entire Wise Ink Creative Publishing family for guiding me in publishing this book.

Thanks to my editors Andrew Wetzel and Rebecca Wheelock for their belief in this project, their patience, and hard work. A special thanks to my creative team, Jessie Bright for the cover design, Kim Morehead for the interior design, Jany Banez for the photo, and Emily Shaffer Rodvold for the web design. I must also thank my mother, brothers, sister, Alpart/Bonjean family, and the Cooper's for allowing this story to be told. Huge thanks to the Manley Crew coaches, staff, and teammates who are all heroes in this story.

A number of dear friends walked this journey alongside me and has given their time, talent, and treasure. A heart felt thanks goes to Alvin Ross, Kimble Singleton, Juan Greer, DJ Mike Strick, Chee-Yun Kim, Ida Spigseth, Melvin Tann, Dennis Rittenmeyer, Leslie Rittenmeyer, Aunt Tina, Tim Fields, Rene Fields, Preston Grandberry, Adam Lowder, Steven Smith, Andrew Ravin, Min Kim, Lila Leff, Scott Prohaska, Tisha Gonzales, Jayson Leisenring, the Goodman/Bagaloo family, and especially Uriah Hall and Arnold Castillo.

I would like to thank Michael Meacham who was there when this idea was birth and helped non-stop. Without the legal and generous help of Jennifer Bonjean, not sure if this book would have happened. I am eternally grateful to Stacy Bagaloo, who been by my side from beginning to end. You are my motivation.

Last and not least: I will like to thank God, and I ask for forgiveness of all those who have been with me over the course of the years and names I have failed to mention.